AUTHENTIC
FENG SHUI©

AUTHENTIC
FENG SHUI©

Practical
Geomantic Analysis
for
Modern Living

THE AUTHOR
REV. VICTORIO HUA WONG SENG TIAN
Professor, Oriental Research Center
Grand Minister, Sheng Lian Temple
Founder, Sheng Lian Charity Clinic

EASTERN Dragon PRESS

Published by:
Eastern Dragon Books 1993
Reprint 1995
A Division of S. Abdul Majeed & Co.
7, Jalan 3/82, Bangsar Utama,
Off Jalan Bangsar,
59000 Kuala Lumpur, Malaysia

© *Rev. Victorio Hua Wong Seng Tian*

ISBN 983-899-213-5

Printed by : Percetakan Sooriya.

THE AUTHOR
REV. VICTORIO HUA WONGSENGTIAN

ABOUT THE AUTHOR

Reverend Victorio Hua WongSengTian is a Taoist Grand Minister at Sheng Lian Temple in Quezon City,Even as a young boy, he has shown extraordinary psychic abilities and was instructed in the writings and practices of Taoism by a Taoist Grand Minister in China.

The Reverend is probably the foremost feng shui expert in the Philippines today. His method of assessing feng shui is more intuitive than technical as he possesses the unique ability of being able to recognize and detect ch'i, which is the most important component of feng shui. Briefly, ch'i is that vital force which is the life essence and motivating force of all things. He can read and interpret both visible and invisible signs in the environment because his psychic senses have been so keenly developed as to tune in with the surroundings like a short wave radio or antennae.

Thousands of people have come to the Temple to seek his help to obtain favourable feng shui for their homes and offices in order to attain good health, good luck, success, prosperity and happiness.

PREFACE

Feng shui is also called Chinese Geomancy. Although literally feng shui means " **wind** " and " **water** " , it really deals with the workings of mysterious earth forces which are believed to be responsible for determining health, prosperity, and good luck. Feng shui therefore is the art and science of directing, balancing and harmonizing these forces, called ch'i, for the benefit of mankind.

I personally learned feng shui from a Taoist teacher in China. I have been a feng shui practitioner for more than thirty years in the Southeast Asia and have been consulted by thousands of Chinese, Filipinos and other nationalities.

Over these years, my practice has led to the establishment of the Sheng Lian Temple and Sheng Lian Charity Clinic located in Quezon City. It has always been my desire to share my knowledge of feng shui with every one so that they and their descendants may receive the blessings of good health, good luck, success, prosperity and happiness both at home and at work.

The book is divided into two major portions. The first parts deals with a simple discussion of the origin and evolution of feng shui which involve a deep and wide application of Chinese philosophy and thoughts. The latter portion expounds my practice, experience and teachings on the treatment of feng shui in various settings and circumstances.

Finally, I was further inspired to write this book by the interest shown by my fellow Rotarians from various Chapters like the Rotary Club of Metro Sta. Mesa, Rotary Club of Downtown Manila, Rotary Club of Manila East and others, who at one time or another had invited me to discuss with them some basic concepts of feng shui.

I like to take this opportunity to thank all my friends for their support and encouragement. To the readers, I hope you will gain and expand your knowledge in this mystic world of feng shui.

Reverend Victorio Hua WongSengTian

CONTENTS

Part III : Feng Shui About Office

Part IV : Decorations

Part V : Solutions

Part VI : Supernatural

Part VII : Feng Shui Cures

Part VIII : Conclusion

Part IX: Appendix

GLOSSARY

BA - GUA - The eight trigrams or the octagonal symbol of the I-Ching; to which are ascribed eight characteristics relating to nature , human, family relationships, and even areas within the house.

BUDDHISM - One of the three great religions of the world . It was founded some 2,500 years ago by **SAKYAMUNI BUDDHA** - an Indian prince. The religion taught equality and compassion as the means to save humanity and realization of the theory of interpendence as the guides to right thinking.

CH'I - Life - giving force, cosmic breath or energy ascribed to atmosphere, earth and humans.

HSUAN - CHIH - LING - FA - That which is outside the scope of our science range of knowledge; these are the " illogical cures.

LO - PEN - The ruler used in feng shui.

LUO - PAN - A compass with Chinese characters in concentric circles depicting the guidelines used in analyzing the feng shui of a site.

LUO - PAN - TING - KENG - That which is known. This is within our scope of experience and knowledge; these are the "logical cures".

TAO - A philosophical concept of unity of opposites that describes the true nature and harmonious principles governing the biological world and universe.

TAOISM - A religion and a philosophy that existed more than 3,000 years ago. It preaches transcendance of the mundane through identifying oneself with the tao and laws of Nature. Taoism has made contributions in scientific fields such as astronomy. mathematics, geology, cartography, chemistry, minerology and herbal medicine.

TAO TEH CHING - The book by Laotze, which is the most important document in Chinese philosophy. It provides for a complete explanation on the perfect union of human and Heaven.

TIEN - JEN - HO - I Literally means "heaven and man in harmonious union"; to make all people enjoy a peaceful, prosperous life without fear and oppression.

YIN - YANG THEORY - The Taoist concept that unites all opposites.

1. ORIGINS OF FENG SHUI

Feng shui is also called Chinese geomancy. Geomancy is both an art and science which originated from ancient China about some three thousand years ago and was carefully studied, further developed and carried over from generation to generation until today. It is the knowledge of placing or arranging things in correct and proper position or direction so as to harness the living force (called ch'i) of a setting to benefit the lives of people.

The application of feng shui involves things, possessions, and persons as well as places such as a lot, house, room,office or building and even a burial sites.

Feng shui is not superstitious belief and does not contradict the teachings of any religion, customs or traditions. The aim of feng shui practice is to bring about good fortune, good health, prosperity and happiness to the practitioner. It is an eco-art dealing with conversation, ecology, political, geography astronomy, orientation and special arrangement. It parallels terrestrial magnetism, astrophysics, psychology and at times, it is plain good design. Sometimes, feng shui falls short of logical explanations so that it remains a mystery to others.

Feng shui operates on many levels. It covers a vast area of human endeavor, along with directing the destiny of countries, regions, families and individuals. At this point, feng shui can be highly personalized, depending upon the individual needs, desires and criteria. Its philosophical roots covers a whole range of Chinese bible thought "CH'I" from I CHING, which were devised by the Chinese sage, Fu-Hsi, B.C. 3322 and "TAO" from Tao Teh Ching - Laotze's book B.C. 1122. These two books are the key to understanding the silent dialogue between Human and Nature, whispered through the fundamental plasma of the Universe known as "TAO" and a cosmic breath, known as "CH'I", that unseen powers governing the universe and affecting our bodies, minds and fates.

2. CH'I OR COSMIC BREATH

Ch'i is the most important component of feng shui. It is the vital force that breathes life into animals and vegetation, inflates the earth to form mountains, and carries water through the earth's ducts. Ch'i is a life essence, a motivating force. It animates all things. And while all things - hills, streams, trees, humans, animals, and stones inhale ch'i, they also exhale it, thus affecting each other.

Ch'i is a pervasive concept in Chinese traditional arts ranging from acupuncture and medicine to feng shui and kung fu. It can include such diverse phenomena as the energy that moves waves; the source of fertile earth, what martial artists channel when striking powerful blows; what acupuncturists seek to activate with their needles; and even man's aura. Feng shui experts determine the best ch'i flows so that man will live the most healthy, productive, prosperous and happy life,

Ch'i is extensive and vague. Yet it ascends, and descends, and moves in all ways without ever ceasing. A person receive the flow of ch'i from the heaven as well as from the ground of the earth. In Chinese, the character ch'i has two meanings, i.e., one cosmic and one human.   The former encompasses air, steams, gas, weather and force while the latter includes breath, aura, manner and energy. Man's ch'i is strongly influenced by the ch'i of both heaven and earth.

Atmospheric ch'i moulds human ch'i. When ch'i is too far away, no water flows, pollution and sickness thrive, and there will be bad luck. Ch'i must flow smoothly and near a person to improve his ch'i. It must be balanced. If the current is too strong or weak, it can have negative effects.

Ch'i, this breath of life, is man's aura, man's real self, his energy and soul. It can be seen by some people. It propels us through life and affects our interaction with others. Every human movement influences both the self and other people, We are drawn together and repelled as magnets attract and repel. In feng shui, people are also sensitive to the ch'i of their environment. Atmospheric ch'i shapes human ch'i, casting man's destiny. Feng shui practitioners try to direct a smooth, good current of ch'i to a person and divert or convert harmful ch'i.

There are eight general types of ch'i as enumerated below:

1) life-force ch'i   (good)
2) lucky ch'i   (good)
3) smooth ch'i   (good)
4) fluctuating ch'i   (neither good not bad)
5) ch'i from evil force   (bad)
6) unlucky ch'i   (bad)
7) suffocating ch'i   (bad)
8) dead ch'i   (bad)

TABLE 1

EVOLUTION OF THE EIGHT SYMBOLS

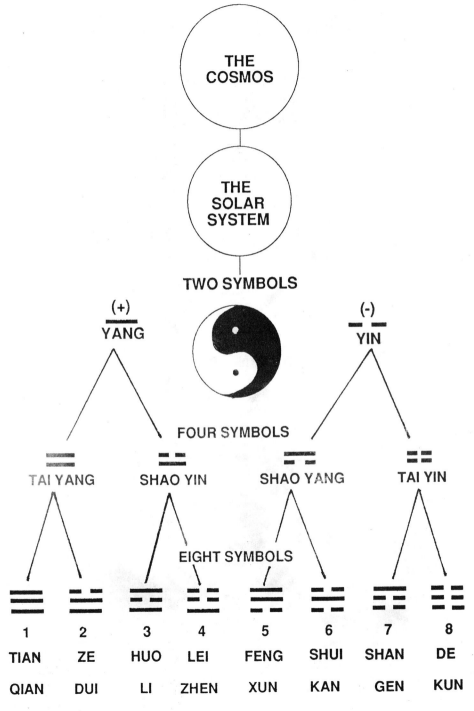

THE
COSMOS

THE
SOLAR
SYSTEM

TWO SYMBOLS

(+)
YANG

(-)
YIN

FOUR SYMBOLS

TAI YANG   SHAO YIN   SHAO YANG   TAI YIN

EIGHT SYMBOLS

1	2	3	4	5	6	7	8
TIAN	ZE	HUO	LEI	FENG	SHUI	SHAN	DE
QIAN	DUI	LI	ZHEN	XUN	KAN	GEN	KUN

TABLE 2

ANCIENT AND MODERN BA-GUA

"ANCIENT BA GUA"

先天八卦

"MODERN BA GUA"

後天八卦

3.   I CHING   AND THE   BA-GUA

For thousands of years the Chinese have based their divination of the future on the working of the I-Ching (or Yi-Ching) or the classic Book of Changes. The I Ching stresses a fundamental Chinese approach: constant cyclical changes. It provides an overview of the universe as an entity and all things in it in constant flux.

Yin and Yang, the two primordial forces that govern the universe, symbolize harmony. They are opposites. Yin is dark, Yang is light; Yin is passive, Yang is active; Yin is female while Yang is male. All things contain varying degrees of Yin and Yang. Yin and Yang continually interact, creating cyclical change. Yin and Yang merge together into one-naturally and constantly creating TAO, the universal situation. The practice of feng shui grew out of both esoteric and popular forms of Taoism.

The I-Ching symbols conjure up cosmic power and energy. The Yang is represented by a continous line ——— and the Yin by a broken line — —   Out of the great extreme symbols of the Yang and Yin come the evolution of the four symbols and the eight trigrams as shown in the diagram. (The eight trigrams further evolved into the sixty-four hexagrams of the I-Ching).

The eight trigrams form is what is commonly known as Ba-gua. There are two types of Ba-gua, one ancient and the other modern Ba-gua.

The ancient Ba-gua carries the original version of the primordial eight trigrams while the modern Ba-gua depicts a rearrangement of the ancient version and incorporates in the

TABLE 3

RELATIONSHIP OF MODERN BA-GUA AND THE FIVE ELEMENTS

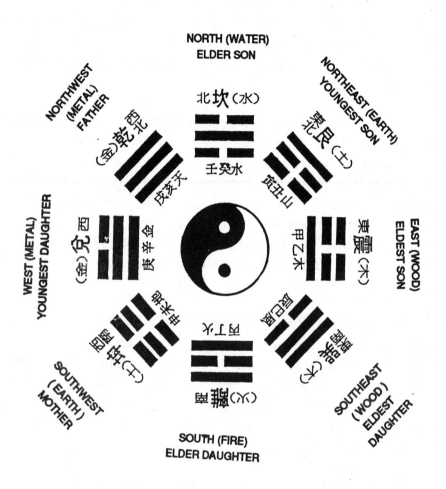

Ba-gua directions the four seasons, month, time, colors with their respective elements of nature and the corresponding family members.

TABLE 4

"BA GUA" WITH THEIR CORRESPONDING
RELATION TO THE MEMBERS OF THE FAMILY

SYMBOL	NO	EMBLEM	ORIENTATION	ELEMENT SIGN	FAMILY RELATIONSHIP
☰	1	HEAVEN	NW	METAL	FATHER
☱	2	LAKE	W	METAL	YOUNGEST DAUGHTER
☲	3	FIRE	S	FIRE	ELDER DAUGHTER
☳	4	THUNDER	E	WOOD	ELDEST SON
☴	5	WIND	SE	WOOD	ELDEST DAUGHTER
☵	6	WATER	N	WATER	ELDER SON
☶	7	MOUNTAIN	NE	EARTH	YOUNGEST SON
☷	8	LAND	SW	EARTH	MOTHER

4. THE FIVE ELEMENTS

More than 3,000 years ago, the Chinese had already established the order of the Five Elements (wood, earth, fire, water and metal), which are powers or essences describing all matters and attributes. These five elements are manifestations arising out of the interplay of Yin and Yang.

The five elements have relative effects on each other, creating and destroying one another in a fixed succession. The productive cycle goes this way: fire produces earth (ash), earth produces metal, metal creates water (smelting, liquification and evaporation), water feeds wood (plant or tree needs water to grow), and wood aids fire (by burning).

Fire - Earth - Metal - Water - Wood - Fire

The chain of destruction is: wood harms earth (wood being dug into the earth), earth obstruct water (by absorbing water) water destroys fire, fire metal and metal chop down wood.

Wood - Earth - Water - Fire - Metal - Wood

The Chinese also associate these elements with time, space, matter, senses, colors and psychological moods. For example, the corresponding directions, seasons and colors are assign to each element as follows :

TABLE 5

THE FIVE ELEMENTS

METAL   WOOD

EARTH   FIRE   WATER

TABLE 6

THE CYCLES OF THE FIVE ELEMENTS

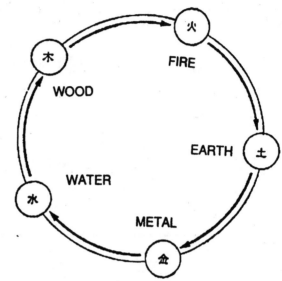

1) PRODUCTIVE CYCLE　五 行 相 生 圖

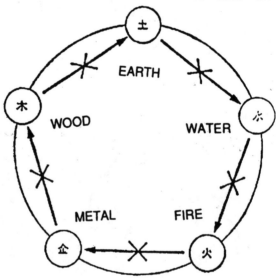

2) DESTRUCTIVE CYCLE　五 行 相 剋 圖

TABLE 7

THE RELATIONSHIPS BETWEEN THE ELEMENTS OF A PERSON AND THAT OF HIS SURROUNDINGS

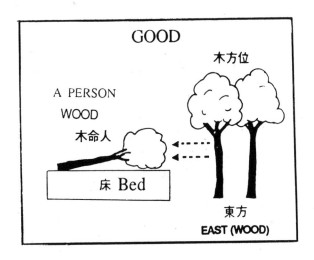

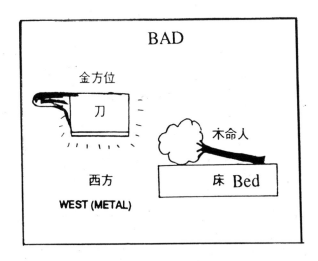

TABLE 8

FENG SHUI COLOR CHART

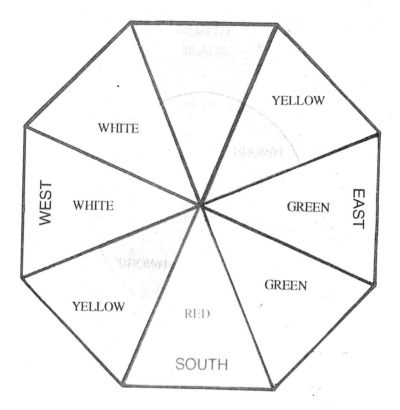

5 ELEMENTS	DIRECTIONS	COLORS
WOOD 木	EAST / SE	GREEN
FIRE 火	SOUTH	RED
EARTH 土	NE / SW	YELLOW/BROWN
METAL 金	WEST / NW	WHITE
WATER 水	NORTH	BLUE/BLACK

TABLE 9
THE FIVE ELEMENTS IN HUMAN ANATOMY

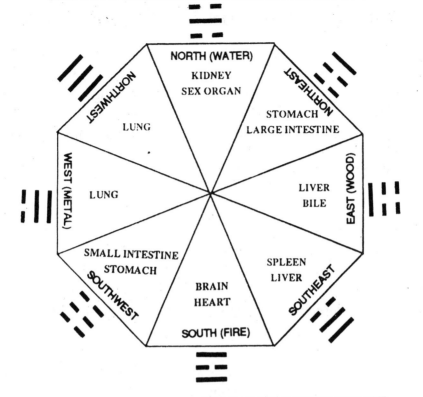

5 ELEMENTS	DIRECTIONS	ORGAN
WOOD	EAST	LIVER/BILE
WOOD	SOUTHEAST	LIVER/SPLEEN
FIRE	SOUTH	HEART/BRAIN
EARTH	NORTHEAST	STOMACH LARGE INTESTINE
EARTH	SOUTHEAST	STOMACH SMALL INTESTINE
METAL	WEAT	LUNG
METAL	NORTHWEST	LUNG
WATER	NORTH	KIDNEY SEX ORGAN

ELEMENT	DIRECTION	SEASON	COLOR
Wood	East	Spring	Green
Fire	South	Summer	Red
Earth	At the center	Mid-Autumn	Yellow/Brown
Metal	West	Autumn	White
Water	North	Winter	Black/Blue

The five elements are also associated with the human anatomy, as follows:

Wood - liver, bile, spleen
Fire - heart, brain
Earth - stomach, large intestine, small intestine
Metal - lung
Water - kidney, sex organ

TABLE 10

THE FIVE ELEMENTS IN RELATION TO THE
10 CELESTIAL STEMS AND 12 BRANCHES

SYMBOL	ELEMENT	COLORED	YIN YANG SIGN	THE CELESTIAL STEMS	THE TERRESTIAL BRANCHES
	WOOD	GREEN	(+)	CHIA	YIN
			(-)	YI	MAO
	FIRE	RED	(+)	PING	WU
			(-)	TING	SZU
	EARTH	YELLOW OR BROWN	(+)	MOU	CHEN
			(+)		HSU
			(-)	CHI	CHOU
			(-)		WEI
	METAL	WHITE	(+)	KENG	SHEN
			(-)	HSIN	YU
	WATER	BLUE OR BLACK	(+)	JEN	TZU
			(-)	KUEI	HAI

5. THE FIVE ELEMENTS AND THE CHINESE 60-YEARS CALENDAR CYCLE

Thousand of years ago, the Imperial Emperor of China instructed scholars to develop the 60-years cosmic cycle of the Chinese calendar as well as the ten celestial stems and twelve terrestrial branches or the Chinese zodiac signs.

The ten stems are: CHIA, YI, PING, TING, MOU, CHI, KENG, HSUN, JEN and KUEI: while the twelve telestial branches or the zodiac signs are: RAT, OX, TIGER, RABBIT, DRAGON, SNAKE, HORSE, GOAT, MONKEY, ROOSTER, DOG and PIG.

The relationship of the five elements, ten celestial stems and the zodiac signs are shown below:

ELEMENT	TEN CELESTIAL STEMS	ZODIAC SIGNS
Wood	Chia	Yin (Tiger)
	Yi	Mao (Rabbit)
Fire	Ping	Wu (Horse)
	Ting	Szu (Snake)
Earth	Mou	Chen (Dragon)
	Chi	Hsu (Dog)
		Chou (Ox)
		Wei (Goat)
Metal	Keng	Shen (Monkey)
	Hsin	Yu (Rooster)
Water	Jen	Tsu (Rat)
	Kuei	Hai (Pig)

TABLE 11

THE 60-YEARS COSMIC CYCLE WITH THE 5 ELEMENTS

6. COMPASS OF FENG SHUI

The world's first compass was invented in China. It is called "LUO-PAN". It is a traditional feng shui tool used for harmonizing the perfection of the universe with the earth.

Luo-pan feature is quite intricate, with all the elements of the universe charted in concentric circles around a lodestone. It's calibration is in Chinese characters and this make it more difficult for laymen to understand.

Since siting with the use of luo-pan is very important and very exacting, the author hereby translates the luo-pan into the modern compass applications as described in the following chart and illustration :

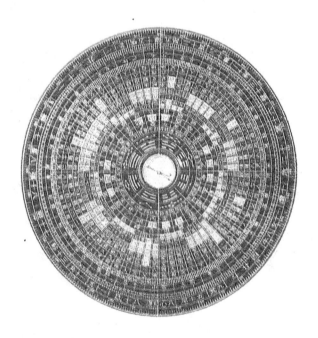

TABLE 12

MODERN 24 MOUNTAINS
WITH EIGHT COMMON DIRECTIONS

TABLE 13

MODERN 24 MOUNTAINS
WITH THEIR DEGREE READING

ORIENTATION		24 DIRECTIONS (CHINESE NAMES)	DENOTED NAME OF 24 DIRECTIONS	DEGREE READING
N O R T H	N. NW.	JEN	9	337.5 - 352.5
	N.	TZU	RAT	352.5 - 7.5
	N. NE.	KUEI	10	7.5 - 22.5
N E	N. NE.	CHOU	OX	22.5 - 37.5
	E.	GEN	N.E.	37.5 - 52.5
	E. S.E.	YIN	TIGER	52.5 - 67.5
E A S T	E. SE.	CHIA	1	67.5 - 82.5
	S.E.	MAO	RABBIT	82.5 - 97.5
	E. SE.	YI	2	97.5 - 112.5
S E	S. SE.	CHEN	DRAGON	112.5 - 127.5
	S. E.	XUN	S.E.	112.5 - 142.5
	S. SE.	SZU	SNAKE	142.5 - 157.5
S O U T H	S. SE.	PING	3	157.5 - 172.5
	S.	WU	HORSE	172.5 - 187.5
	S. SW.	TING	4	187.5 - 202.5
S W	S. SW.	WEI	GOAT	202.5 - 217.5
	S. W.	KUN	S.W.	217.5 - 232.5
	W. SW.	SHEN	MONKEY	232.5 - 247.5
W E S T	W. SW.	KENG	7	247.5 - 262.5
	W.	YU	ROOSTER	262.5 - 277.5
	W. NW.	HSIN	8	277.5 - 292.5
N W	W. NW.	SHII	DOG	292.5 - 307.5
	N. W.	QIAN	N.W.	307.5 - 322.5
	N. NW.	HAI	PIG	322.5 - 337.5

TABLE 14

FOUR FUNDAMENTAL PRINCIPLES OF FENG SHUI

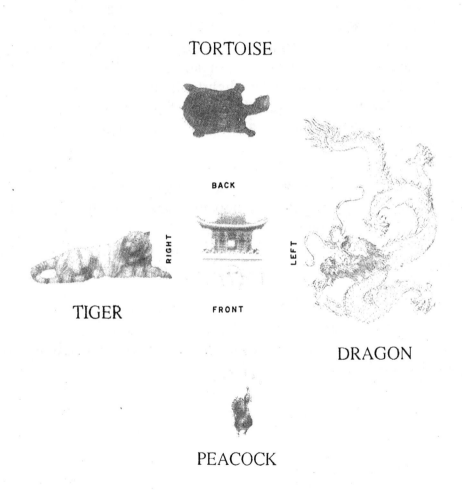

TORTOISE

BACK

RIGHT

LEFT

FRONT

TIGER

DRAGON

PEACOCK

7.   CLASSIC   FENG   SHUI   SITE

Almost all experts agree that the classic or ideal feng shui site is the protective " armchair " hill formation, also known as " dragon-protecting pearl " or " mother embracing child ". This formation is composed of a packed of powerful earthly beasts: the green dragon, the white tiger, the black tortoise and the vermillon phoenix.   The best site for a house and lot is the one facing south and backed by a high (black tortoise) mountain for protection. It is flanked to the right, or west, by the fierce white tiger and to the left, or east, by a slightly higher green dragon, The dragon side should be slightly higher to keep the tiger's appetite away from the site. The lower front, facing south, is the vermillon phoenix side,   a sort of footstool to the armchair formation.

In addition to retaining and emitting their own ch'i, the tortoise, tiger, dragon and phoenix can snare the good ch'i flowing over the phoenix. Ideally a house is build halfway up the black tortoise mountain, which is neither too high nor too low, and looking over the phoenix with a commanding view.

If the ideal setting is not possible, ask a geomancer. He can determine and describe what is needed to be done to restore the balance of all earthly elements so as to achieve harmony and tranquility.

TABLE 15

DIRECTIONS ON USING THE LUO-PAN

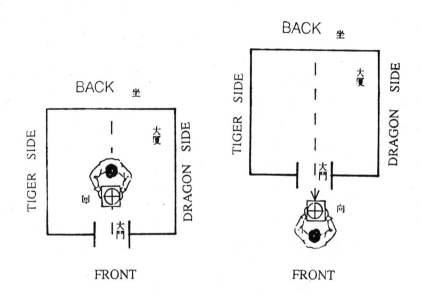

Main House Door

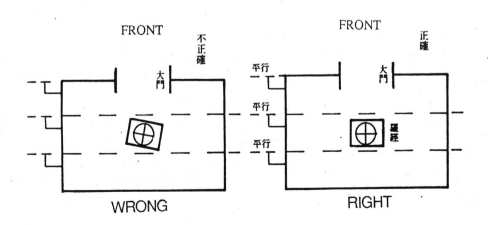

8. POSITIONING, FACING, AND THE CENTERPOINT

In feng shui, the usual discussion revolves around three important points, the positioning of furnitures, the facings of appliances and parts of the house, and the location of the centerpoint of the property.

The arrangement of the furnitures in a room can influence the ch'i of the house. The place could be done artistically and it could be very pleasing to look at, but if the ch'i was not enhanced then the occupants may not be happy living in it.

Likewise, the facings of bed and stove are very important in feng shui. Many people are unclear whether geomantic influence is applied to the facings of the bed or the sleeper's head or the sleeper's feet. Usually, we get confused on the importance of the facings of the stove and that of the cook. These will be discussed in the succeeding chapters for further clarification.

Lastly, the centerpoint of a house is also carefully considered in feng shui discussions. A house with no centerpoint is a place with bad feng shui, because the center of the house is likened to the owner's heart. A man without heart will have no life and energy, it follows then, that the house without centerpoint will have no good luck to offer its occupants. Care for the centerpoint of a place entails cleanliness. Avoid placing post or tree on it, neither should we locate the toilet, kitchen, septic tank or swimming pool on the spot.

The following illustrations will explain how to determine the proper positioning and facing of things, and to locate the centerpoint of a lot or house. However, for accuracy and convenience you may ask professional help to guide you on this matter.

TABLE 16

PARTS OF A HOUSE

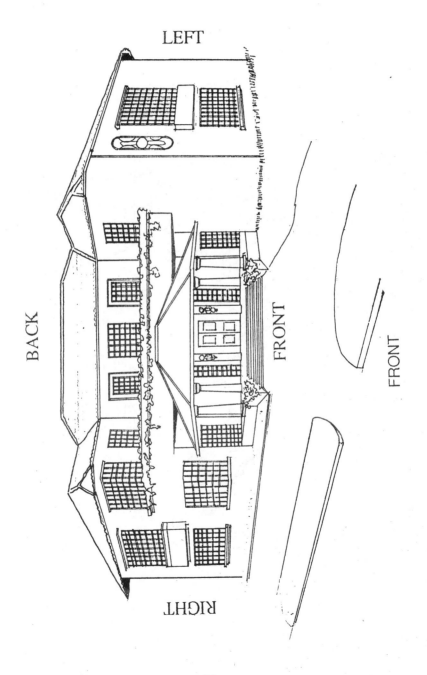

LEFT

BACK

FRONT

FRONT

RIGHT

27

TABLE 17

POSITION OF A DOOR

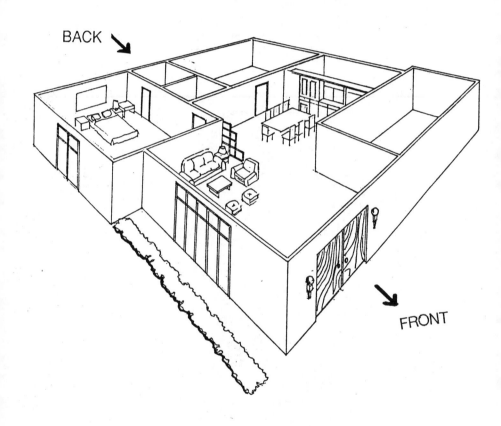

BACK

FRONT

TABLE 18
THE FACINGS OF A BED

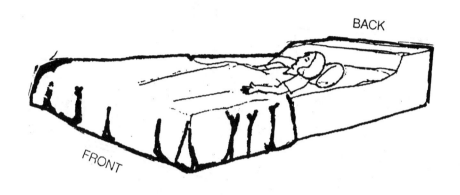

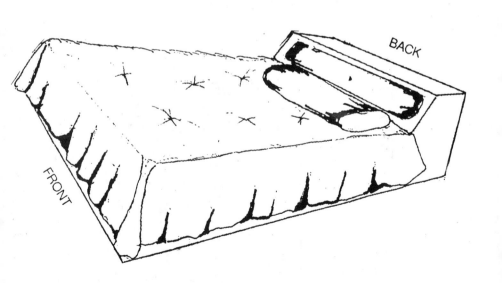

TABLE 19

THE FACINGS OF STOVE AND RANGE

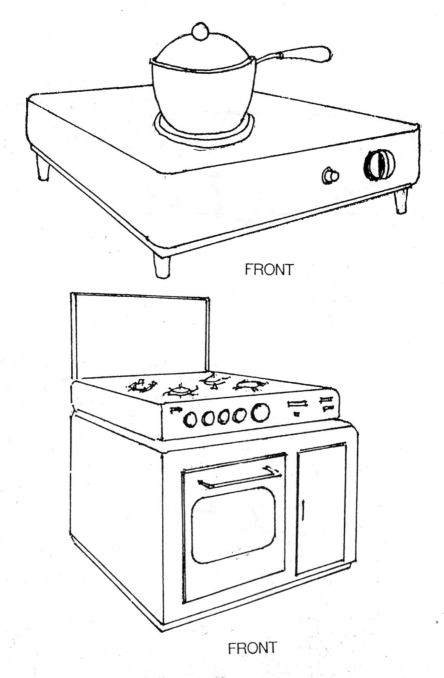

FRONT

FRONT

THE CENTERPOINT OF A PLACE

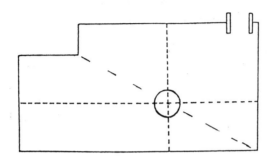

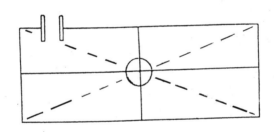

WITH   CENTERPOINT

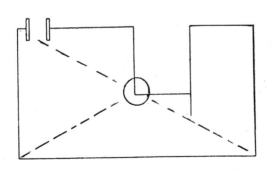

WITHOUT   CENTERPOINT

HANABISHI®

Safety is our Guarantee

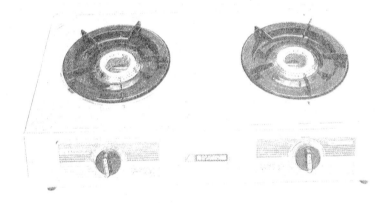

STOVE FRONT ALWAYS REFERS TO THE FACE WITH SWITCH KNOB

10.   SHAPES   AND   TERRAINS

The shape of the house with either protrusions or hollow parts have certain geomantic implications on the occupants depending on the location, as follows:

NORTH   protruded - can easily acquire friends; hollow - will meet accidents. It is best not to have protrusions or hollow parts in this direction.

NORTHEAST   protruded - likes to research and experiment; hollow - lacks planning in work.

EAST   protruded - daring and will undertake risky ventures, impatient ;   hollow - easily discouraged.

SOUTHEAST   protruded - need to exert much effort in work; hollow - daughters will have unsuccessful love affairs.

SOUTH   protruded - will have good reputation; hollow - will meet bad friends.

SOUTHWEST   protruded - female members will be active while the males will be lazy; hollow - will have bad luck.

WEST   protruded - family will be happy; hollow - family members will have tendency to flirt.

NORTHWEST   protruded - likes to compete; hollow - tend to be quarrelsome.

Houses with too much protrusions or hollow parts can also evoke the following readings deduced from the Ba-gua:

NORTH   son wants to be the leader at all times; may suffer from kidney and urinary tract problems; may have business failure.

NORTHEAST   son does not readily accepts defeat and may suffer from abdominal problems and meet many obstructions.

EAST   son may suffer from Hepatitis, meet obstruction and lose wealth.

SOUTHEAST   daughter may suffer from Hepatitis, lose wealth and be childless.

SOUTH   daughter may suffer from heart problem, be involve in family quarrels and meet obstruction.

SOUTHWEST   mother may suffer from abdominal problems

TABLE 21

THE FAVORABLE SHAPES OF LOT

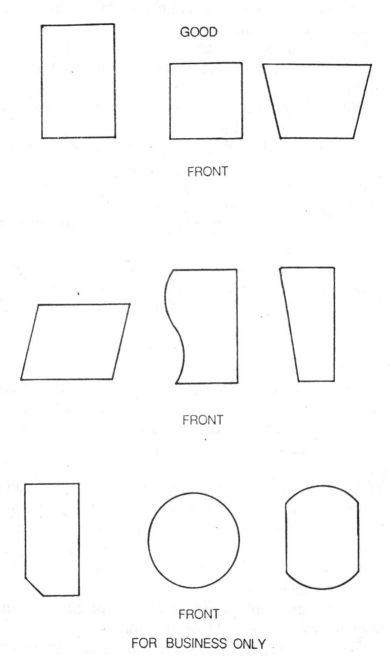

GOOD

FRONT

FRONT

FRONT

FOR BUSINESS ONLY

TABLE 22

THE UNFAVORABLE SHAPES OF LOT

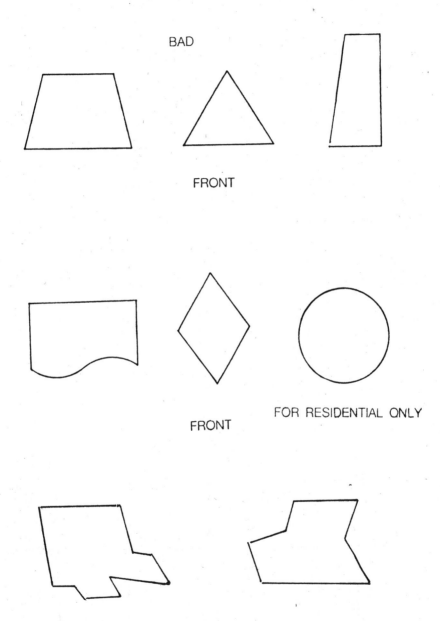

BAD

FRONT

FRONT

FOR RESIDENTIAL ONLY

FRONT

TABLE 23

SHAPES THAT SHOULD BE AVOIDED

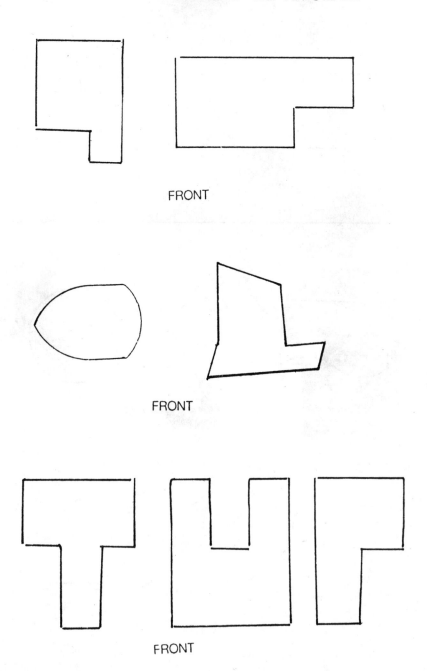

FRONT

FRONT

FRONT

and meet obstruction.

WEST   daughter will suffer from respiratory problems, be unlucky and meet obstruction.

NORTHWEST   father will suffer from respiratory problems, be unlucky and meet obstruction.

However, it should be mentioned that protrusions or hollow parts not exceeding one -third the length or dimension of that given side will not be affected by the above geomantic implications or readings.

Before buying a lot, individual features of the land must be considered. The best shapes are either square or rectangular. Avoid odd - angled plot, because irregular shapes can mean trouble. It has adverse influence on health and can indirectly affect fortune, too. For rectangular lot with unusually long length, care must be exercised during construction to avoid the influence of bad ch'i, L - shape and dust pan shapes should be avoided.   Shapes with many corners or triangular are unfavourable.

Observe the terrain of the lot. Level or flat terrain is most favourable; while a terrain shaped like a wok, ascertains that there will be no flooding.

Elevation or depression on one side of the terrain have the following implications :

EAST   elevation - slow progress; depression - fast and progressive specially if area is wide.

SOUTH   elevation - prone to illness;   depression - helps develop intelligence.

WEST   elevation - enhance cooperation; depression - family members do not have good regard towards each other.

NORTH   elevation - will acquire many friends; depression - money will be spent liberally.

TABLE 24

PROTRUSIONS IN SHAPE OF A CERTAIN LOT

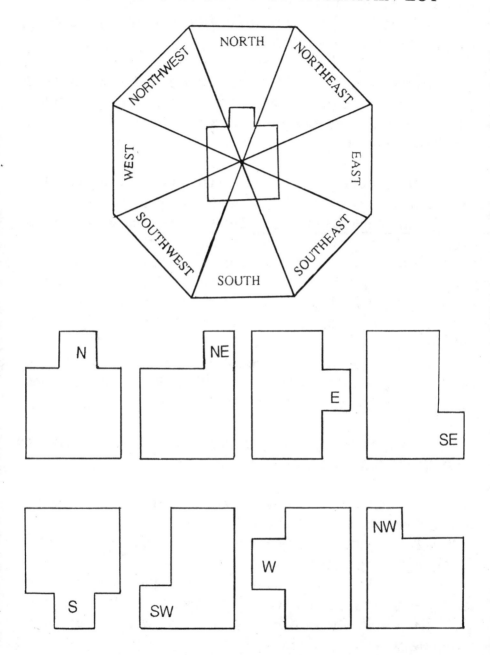

TABLE 25
HOLLOWNESS IN SHAPE OF A CERTAIN LOT

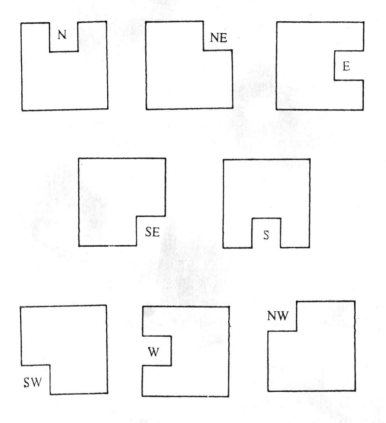

11. EXTERNAL FACTORS OF HOUSE OR BUILDING

External factors affect not only a person's character but can also threaten an area's prosperity. The bend of a river, the shape of an over-pass, or the size, shape and angle of a building's corner can destroy the harmony of good ch'i. Because of this, house planning and awareness of the external conditions are important.

The following feng shui guidelines apply to external factors affecting a house or building:

1. a T or Y-shaped road fronting the house is bad.
2. a house located at the dead-end of a road is unfavourable.
3. an inverted U-shaped road or river in front of the house is unfavourable.
4. house should not face a funeral parlor or cemetery.
5. house should not face a church or temple.
6. house should not face a chimney or water storage tank.
7. a big tree or electric post facing the house is bad.
8. house should not face hospital or police station.
9. roof corner of neighbor's house pointing towards house is unfavourable
10. a canal or river at the back of the house is unfavourable.
11. avoid locating a house beside an overpass.
12. house should not face a bridge.
13. in case of doubt, it is advisable to consult a feng shui expert at the earliest stage to avoid unnecessary expenses.
14. house located at a scenic environment is favourable.

1. House facing a T-shaped road is unfavorable.

住宅最忌路沖。

2. House fronting a Y-junction is unfavorable.

住宅建在如圖所示之處，凶。

3. House facing the neighbor's chimney is unfavorable.

住宅對著煙囪，凶。

4. Main door of house facing a big tree is bad.

住宅前有陰森古樹，易引邪。

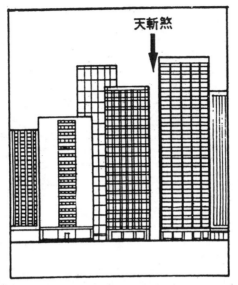

5. House should not be located opposite the "gap" between two buildings.

住宅面對天斬煞，主凶。

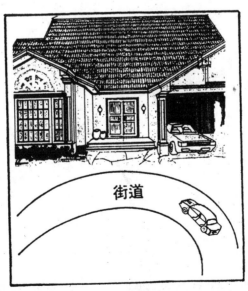

6. Inverted U-shaped road in front of a house is bad.

住宅面向街道反弓處，凶。

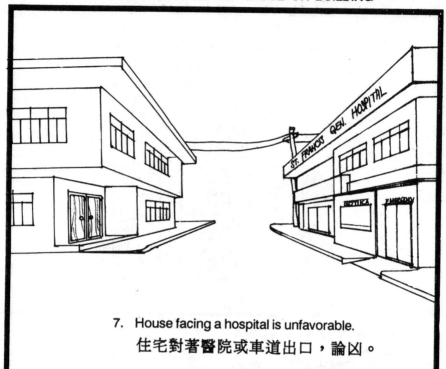

7. House facing a hospital is unfavorable.

   住宅對著醫院或車道出口，論凶。

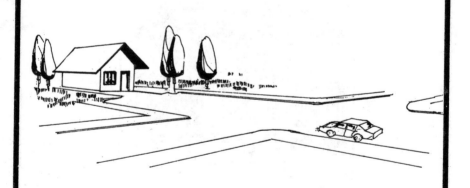

8. A house located at the dead end of a road is unfavorable.

   住宅在死巷盡頭，凶。

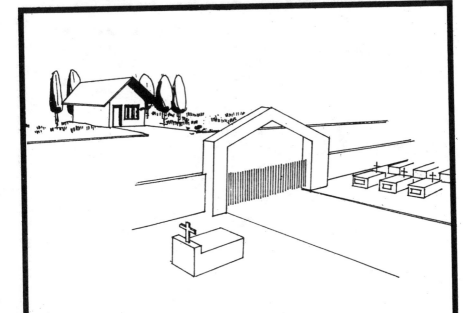

9. House in front of a cemetery is unfavorable.
住宅對著墳場、祠堂，主凶。

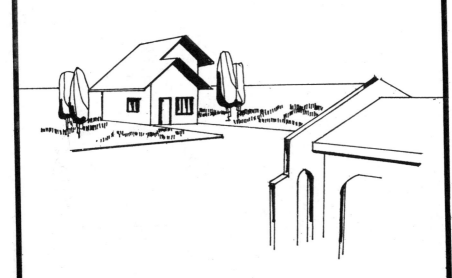

10. House facing a funeral parlor is unfavorable.
住宅對著殯儀館，主凶。

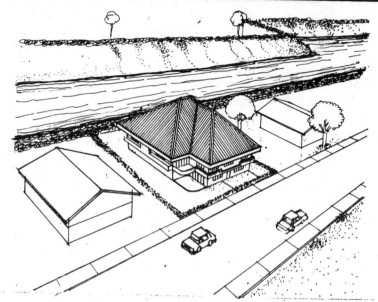

11. A river at the back of the house is bad.

住宅後面有溪流河道，凶。

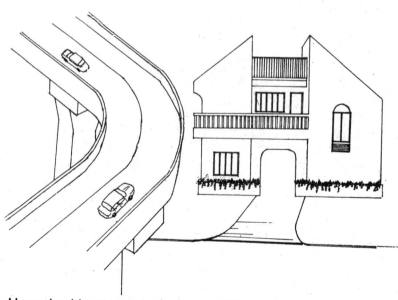

12. House beside an overpass curve or LRT rail with the bulk side facing the house is unfavorable.

住宅在高架車路轉彎處，凶。

12. INTERNAL FACTORS OF HOUSE OR BUILDING

A feng shui expert sees direct relation between the house shape and the destiny, welfare and behavioural pattern of its occupants. The house is the base of family member's life. Determining and shaping ch'i, interiors with good arrangement will nourish the residents' ch'i, to make them thrive in the society and be able to handle hostile circumstances ranging from the mild to the serious ones.

Some general feng shui rules regarding internal factors affecting a house or building are as follows :

1. house or building should not be constructed on a site which used to be a funeral parlor, cemetery or area where massacre happened.
2. avoid having a pond in the center of the house.
3. an opening or a window in the center of the house is unfavourable.
4. having a fire place in the center of the house is bad.
5. toilet should not be located in the center of the house.
6. floor level of the house should not be lower than the road.
7. public drainage pipe should not pass under the house.
8. roof of the house should not be too steep.
9. the walls should not have protrusions or hallow parts.
10. house should not be too stuffy or too dark.
11. dragon side of the house should be higher than the tiger side.
12. additional building or structure at the back side should not be lower than the house.
13. a U-shape house is not advisable.
14. water tank at the center point of a lot or a house is unfavourable.

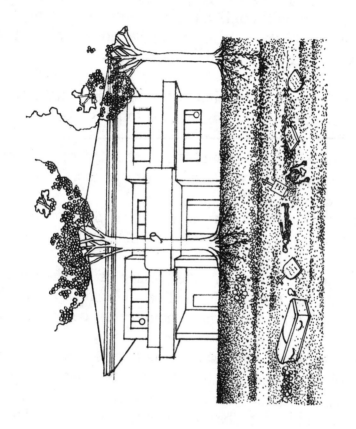

16. House located on former site of cemetery is unfavorable.

住宅建在前為墳場之地為凶。

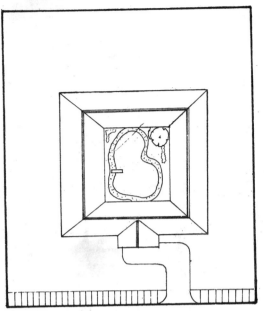

17. Avoid having a pond in the center of the house.

住宅中心點上有水池，凶。

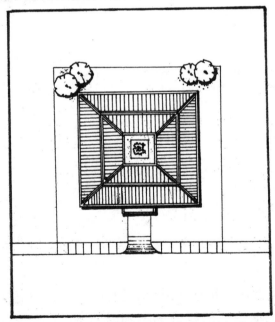

18. An opening in the center of the house is unfavorable.

住宅中心點有天井，凶。

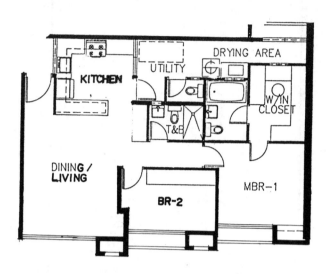

19. Toilet located in the center of the house is bad.

住宅中心設浴廁，大凶。

20. Floor level of the house should be higher than the road

住宅地板比街路低，不利財運。

21. Public drainage pipe passing underneath the house is unfavorable.

溪水或公共臭水流經住宅，凶。

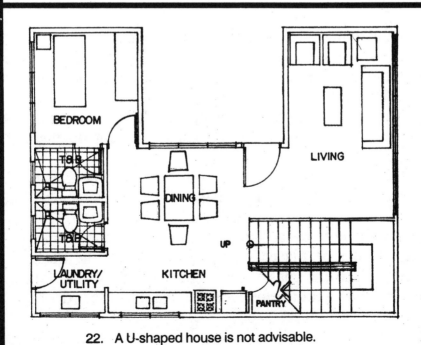

22. A U-shaped house is not advisable.

住宅設計成凹形，主凶。

13.   FENCE, GATE, AND GARAGE

The fence is the boundary that separates the house from the outside world. Upon entering a place, it is good omen to feel refresh, comfortable, and lighthearted. This implies that the place's ch'i is flowing smoothly and everything is well coordinated.

Usually,   the following are observed with regards to height, range and orientation of the fence:

1. fence or property wall should not be too close to the house.
2. fence or property wall should not be higher than the house.
3. avoid having fence with varying height.
4. fence with sharp points towards the house is not advisable.

Main gate's feng shui on the other hand has the following guidelines:

1. it should not be covered with poison vines.
2. installing barbed wire roll over the gate is unfavourable.
3. the slates of gate should be positioned vertically and not horizontally.
4. if there is a small gate beside the main one, the roofs of both gates should not have thorny plants growing on them.

Garage is another part of the house that should be considered carefully.   The major points to remember are:

1. this should not be located on top of the septic tank.
2. it should not be placed on the tiger side of the house.
3. do not place the master bedroom on top of the garage.
4. the driveway should not face the main house's door.

23. Fence or property wall built too close to the house is bad.

圍牆緊迫住宅，凶。

24. Fence higher than the house is not good.

圍牆高過房屋，凶。

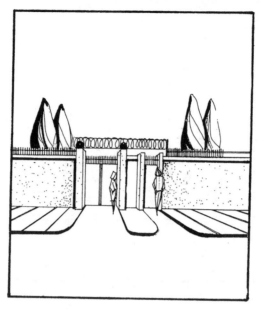

27. Avoid installing barbed wire roll over the gate.

圍牆上鐵絲網忌架在大門上。

28. Gate covered up with poison vines is bad.

藤類植物把圍牆之門纏著，主凶。

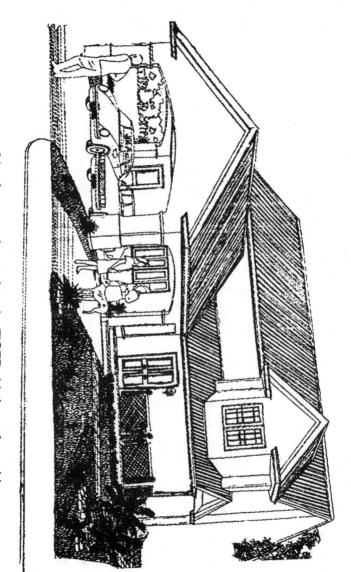

31. A garage located on the TIGER side is not favorable.

車庫不宜設置於住宅白虎方位。

14.   THE MAIN HOUSE DOOR

Many people believe that the main house door or front door should face east or south and should not face northeast or the tiger side of the house. However, most do not know the reasons behind these beliefs. The explanations usually given are as follows:

Facing EAST -   the ultra-violet ray from the morning sun is just right while the ultra-violet ray at noon or afternoon is too strong.

Facing SOUTH -   the flow of wind from the south is gradual and smooth while the sudden wind flow or gust will scatter the ch'i in the house.

Facing NORTHEAST - this is the orientation of evil spirits and hence under the influence of bad ch'i, also called SHA CH'I.

Facing the Tiger Side - it is best that the mouth of the tiger is closed.   Opening and closing door to wards tiger side may influence movement of tiger's mouth and bring about health problems or bad fortune.

The eight general locations for the main door can attract either good or bad feng shui as enumerated below:

Life-force ch'i :   money, fame, health and prosperity.

Lucky ch'i :   successful accomplishment, peaceful, and happy family.

Smooth ch'i :   will meet good friends, have obedient children, family will be happy.

Fluctuating ch'i :   happy family, success will come gradually not suddenly.

Unlucky ch'i :   minor arguments among family members, money will come and go easily.

Evil ch'i :   accidents and poor health are indicated.

Suffocating ch'i :   frequent arguments, quarrels and loss of respect among family members, money often misplaced or lost.

Note: The characteristics of the chi is one of the subject of Feng Shui digest.

Dead ch'i :   everything will be unsuccessful, there's bad
                     fortune, death of offspring during delivery
                     or at early age.

For good feng shui, the orientation of the house and lot should also be compatible with the birthdate of the breadwinner. The best situation is compatibility with both husband and wife.

The following eight feng shui rules apply to the exterior of the main door:

1. main door should not face gate.
2. main door should not face tree or post.
3. main door should not face the neighbor's corner, chimney, or water storage tank.
4. main door should not face a Y-shape road.
5. main door should not face a T- shape road.
6. main door should not face the cross of a church, a funeral parlor or a police station.
7. main door should not face a neighbor's gate, main door or driveway.
8. main door should not face the septic tank.

The following apply to the interior of the main door :

1. main door should not face a staircase.
2. main door should not face a corner.
3. main door should not face a post.
4. main door should not be blocked by a wall; this can confine good ch'i.
5. main door should not face the back door.
6. main door should not face a wash basin, sink or pipe from the water pump.
7. main door should not face the door of any bedroom.
8. upon entering the main door, toilet water closet, stove or the fireplace should be out of view.

Other guidelines relating to the main door are as follows:

1. the back door must be smaller than the main door.
2. the main door should be in line with the wall and not extending in or out.
3. consult a geomancer relating to the proper measurement of the main door.
4. size of the main door should be proportional to the size of the house.
5. design of the lamps outside the main door should be in harmony to the house's design.
6. a house should not have three front doors lined horizontally.
7. main door should not face the door of the sitting room.
8. if the main door is made of two panels, the parts must be of equal sizes.
9. bury " **Five Lucky Objects** " under the inner floor of the main door.
10. main door should not have many parts or too much designs.

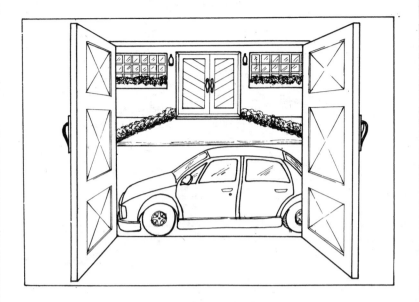

32. A main door facing the neighbor's main door is unfavorable.

大門忌對著人家之大門。

33. A main door facing the gate is unfavorable.

大門忌對著圍牆之門。

34. A main door facing a post is bad.
大門對著電線桿，凶。

35. Main door facing a neighbor's corner is unfavorable.
大門對著人家之屋角，凶。

36. Main door facing a funeral parlor is bad.

大門對著殯儀館，主凶。

37. Main door facing the post of a house is bad.

一入門，對著柱，凶。

38. Main door facing a staircase is unfavorable.
一入門，對著樓梯，凶。

39. Upon entering main door, toilet water closet shoud be out of view.
一入門，看見廁所，凶。

40. Main door facing a corner is bad.

一入門，對著房間尖角，凶。

41. Main door facing the door of any bedroom is bad.

一入門，對著房門，凶。

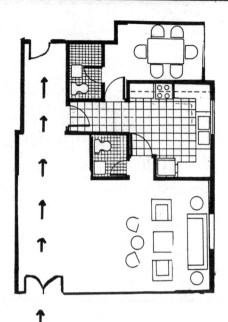

42. Main door and back door forming a straight line is unfavorable.

大門對著後門，凶。

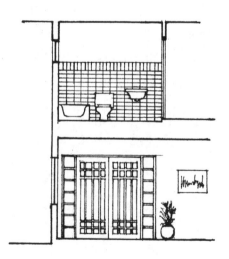

43. Toilet should not be placed above the main door.

大門上面設廁，主凶。

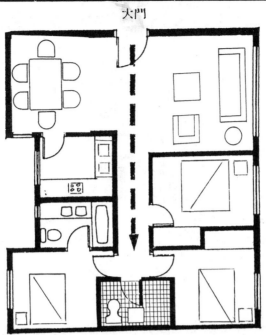

44. Main door directly opposite the toilet is unfavorable.
大門對著浴廁，主凶。

45. The main door should be aligned with the wall.
大門必須和屋向呈直角或同向，方論吉。

46. A series of doors in a line is very unfavorable.

大門忌與其他門成一直線。

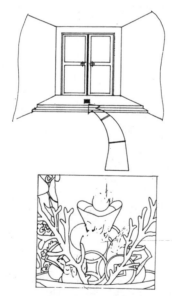

47. It is advisable to bury "5 lucky objects" under the inner floor of a main door.

在大門處，擇吉日藏埋「五寶」，有招財引福之益。

15. ON DESIGNING THE LIVING ROOM

The living or sitting room is the place where family usually gather together or where guests are entertained. It affects the wealth, reputation and cooperation of the house occupants.

The feng shui rules regarding the four general shapes of the living room are as follows:

1. Square shape - there should be no window directly facing the main door; do not place any tall cabinet beside the door; there should be no obstructions along the interior or exterior portion of the main door; avoid ceiling with too many corners.
2. Long and Narrow shape - must be well lighted; do not place chairs beside the main door; putting mirrors on the wall along the longer side is favorable; if the tiles of the floor are rectangular, the longer side should be laid horizontally.
3. Wide and Narrow shape -it is advisable to place chairs beside the main door; putting mirrors on the wall along the wider side is favorable; do not hang pictures or painting depicting odd subjects; it is best that the surface of the ceiling is even, i.e., no protrusions or hollow portion.
4. Round shape - the ceiling should have no mirrors nor many corners; tables should have similar shapes; exposed posts should be covered.

A living room with good feng shui is one that is well lighted, has good ch'i movement and imparts a happy feeling to its occupants. The following ten points should be observed:

1. it must be well lighted.
2. the size should be in proportion to other parts of the house.

3. cover all exposed ceiling beams.
4. ceiling should not be designed with too many corners.
5. the living room should not be crowded with too many furnitures or overly decorated.
6. the color and design of the wall paper should be compatible with the owner's elements.
7. avoid walls with protrusions or hollow portions and dark colored tiles.
8. it is best to have round lamps or chandeliers.
9. ceiling should have no mirrors.
10. floor level should not be lower than that of the house.

It is important to know that every living rooms has a "lucky spot". A geomancer can detect this spot as well as enhance the luck from this spot for the benefit of the occupants. As a rule of thumb, the general location of the lucky spot is related to the facing of the main door.

Here are some suggestions to enhance the good feng shui from the lucky spot:

1. bury "Five Lucky Objects" in the spot.
2. lucky spot should be provided with good lighting.
3. place live plant with soil on the lucky spot.
4. hang an amulet like i.e. lucky 8-treasures, on the wall of the lucky spot.
5. the spot and it's surrounding must be kept clean.

We can maintain the good ch'i from the lucky spot by observing the following:

1. do not place heavy object on the lucky spot.
2. do not place an aquarium on the lucky spot.
3. the back side of the spot should have no window.
4. there should be no ceiling beam on top of the lucky spot.
5. do not place garbage can, shoes, or slipper on the lucky spot.

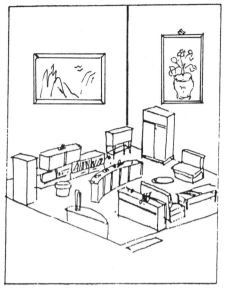

48. A living room with sunlight passing through it's window is very favorable.
客廳沒有窗戶，不吉。

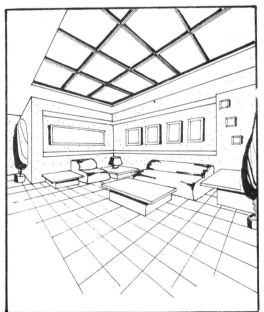

49. The size of the living room should be proportionate to the other parts of the house.
客廳的空間忌太窄或太闊，適度爲佳。

50. Living room with exposed beams on it's ceilings is unfavorable.
客廳的天花板，最忌橫樑突出。

51. Avoid too many corners or rafters on the ceiling of the living room.
客廳的天花板，最忌尖角複雜。

52. Living room must not be crowded with too much furnitures.

客廳必須動線流暢，忌雜亂。

53. Avoid walls with protrusions and dark colored tiles on the living room.

客廳的氣氛宜生氣蓬勃，忌陰森。

54. The ceiling of a living room should not have mirrors.
客廳的天花板不宜安置鏡。

55. Floor level of a living room should not be lower than the floor level of the house.
客廳的地板忌凹陷。

56. It is very auspicious to hang the "Lucky-8-Treasures®" on the living room.

客廳最宜懸掛吉祥靈寶如「八寶靈卦」，可令家運興旺。

57. The main staircase in the living room should not be spiral.

客廳不宜用螺旋狀樓梯。

58.   Bury five lucky objects in the "Lucky Spot".

財位上宜秘藏「五寶」。

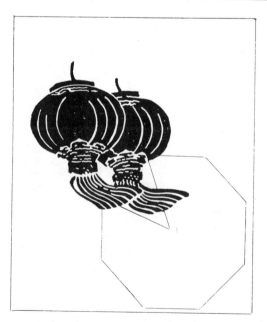

59.   "Lucky spot" should be provided with good lighting.

財位上宜明亮光彩。

60. Place live plant with soil on the "Lucky Spot".

財位上宜生機茂盛。

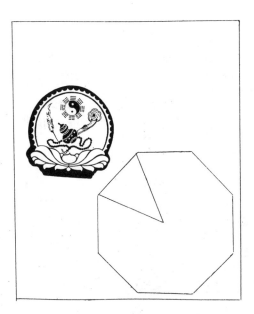

61. Hang the "Lucky-8-Treasures" on the wall of the "Lucky Spot".

財位上宜擺掛吉祥靈寶如「八寶靈卦」。

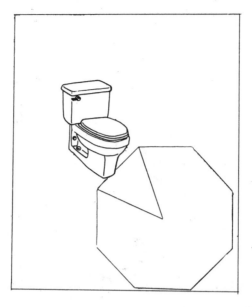

62. A toilet bowl on the "Lucky Spot" is unfavorable.

財位上宜清潔。

63. Placing heavy object on the "Lucky Spot" is unfavorable.

財位上不可雜物疊壓。

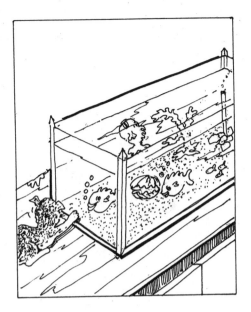

64. Placing an aquarium on the "Lucky Spot" is unfavorable.

財位上不可擺置魚缸。

65. The back side of the "Lucky Spot" should not have a door or window.

財位上最忌缺陷。

66. A post on the "Lucky Spot" is unfavorable.

財位上最忌有橫樑直柱。

67. The "Lucky Spot" should not be dirty.

財位上不可雜亂無章。

16.   MASTER BEDROOM

It is important that the master bedroom of the husband and wife which may also include a dressing room and a toilet and bathroom should be properly positioned so as to attract good feng shui.

The eight general facings for the master bedroom with either good or bad ch'i are as follows:

Life-force ch'i :   couple will be close,   loving, successful and happy.

Lucky ch'i :   couple will understand each other well and the family will be happy.

Smooth ch'i ;   couple will strive to work and do things together.

Fluctuating ch'i : couple will be loving but each will keep secrets from the other.

Unlucky ch'i :   couple will work together but the success of their effort is uncertain.

Evil ch'i :   couple will work together but their efforts will always result in failure.

Suffocating ch'i : couple will be loving but one of them will often encounter health problems.

Dead ch'i :   couple will frequently quarrel, their love for each other will gradually diminish until such time when they will not mind each other anymore and stop communicating.

Generally, it is easier to attract the vital force or good ch'i for a master bedroom that is located on the ground floor as compared to one located upstair. Nevertheless , in either cases, consult a geomancer to be sure that good ch'i flows in the bedroom. With good ch'i, couple can expect to be alert, healthy, have many children and prosper. Scattered or bad ch'i in the master bedroom can result to drowsiness, poor health, few or no children and difficulty in earning a livelihood.

Following are guidelines regarding the master bed and other features:

THE BEDROOM

1. the roof should not have any opening emitting light into the master bedroom.
2. there should be no round windows.
3. ceiling should not have overly unproportional design.
4. the shape should not be irregular or with too many corners.
5. the floor should not be lower than that of the toilet.
6. shelves in the master bedroom is not advisable.
7. there should be no paintings or picture relating to water scenery.
8. do not put an aquarium in the master bedroom.

THE BEDROOM DOOR

1. door should not face a mirror.
2. it should not face a corner.
3. it should not face the door of another room.
4. it should not face the toilet door.
5. it should preferably open towards the dragon side.
6. it should not face the staircase.

THE DRESSER

1. it should not face the door of your bedroom.
2. it should not be placed on both ends of the bed.
3. it should not be placed under the beam or next to a post.
4. it should not face the comfort room.
5. it should not face another mirror.

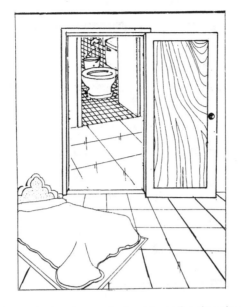

68. The door of a bedroom facing the toilet door is unfavorable.

臥室之門對著浴廁，凶。

69. Door of two bedroom facing each other is bad.

兩間臥室之門相對，凶。

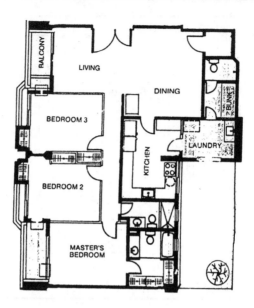

70. Bedroom door facing the main door is bad.

臥室門對著大門，凶。

71. Bedroom door facing a corner is bad.

臥室門對著房角，論凶。

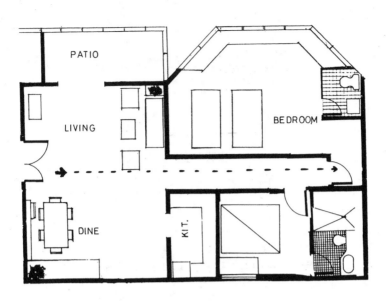

72. Bedroom door facing a long hallway is bad.
臥室在走廊盡頭為凶。

73. Bedroom door facing the staircase is unfavorable.
臥室之門對著樓梯，凶。

74. The ceiling of bedrooms with overly unproportional design is bad.
臥室之天花板忌凸凹角度複雜。

75. The roof of a bedroom should not have any opening or window.
臥室不可開天窗。

76. Bedroom should not have round window.

   臥室不可設圓形窗戶。

77. Flower or plant is not to be displayed in random within the bedroom.

   臥室擺置盆景，必須留意方位。

84. Dresser facing the bed is bad.

梳妝桌忌對床。

17. OTHER BEDROOMS

The following feng shui guidelines apply to the bedrooms for elderly and children:

1. rooms for elderly person should be located at the western or southern side.
2. room for elderly person should not be dark; it should have window.
3. locating children's room at the back of the kitchen is unfavorable.
4. rectangular or square shaped room for the children is ideal; avoid room with too many sides.
5. Sharp object such as sword should not be displayed in the children's room.
6. display of wild stuffed animals in children's room is bad.
7. location of children's bedroom should be compatible with the children's birthdates.
8. locating children's room in the center of the house is not advisable.
9. colors of the children's room should agree with the children's elements

Three important rules to observe are:

1. the color of the carpet in children's room should not clash with the children's elements nor the element of the room's location.
2. it is advisable to put amulet in the children's room and in the room for elderly person to protect their health.
3. in case two or more persons occupy the same room, the suggestions are -

    sleep in separate beds or put a "**Holy Gourd**®" under the bed if they sleep on one bed.

    the color of the room should be compatible with its occupants. For example, two persons whose elements are wood (green) and metal (white) should avoid using either green or white colors for the room because metal clashes with wood.

Below is a table showing the colors of the different elements, clashing colors and suggested room colors:

ELEMENT/ COLOR	CLASHING COLORS	SUGGESTED ROOM COLOR
Wood/Green	White	Blue
Fire / Red	Black, blue	Green
Earth / Yellow,brown	Green	Red
Metal/White	Red	Yellow
Water/Black,Blue	Yellow,Brown	White

Note: More detailed explanation of color, 5 elements with table are among the subject of the Feng Shui digest.

85. Children's room with a window at the Southeast side is good.

小孩房宜光線充足、空氣流暢。

86. Children's room near the kitchen is unfavorable.

小孩房在廚房附近，凶。

87. Sword and wild stuffed animals should not be used for display in the children's room.

小孩房忌掛獸骨利器。

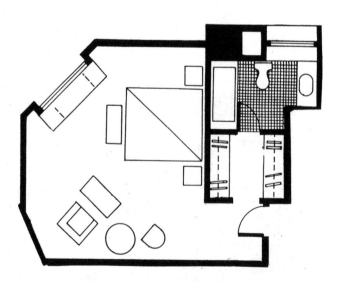

88. Avoid irregular shaped room for children.

小孩房的格局不正，主凶。

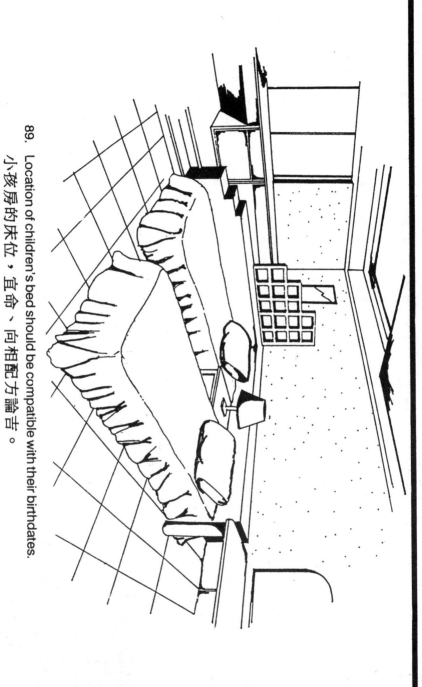

89. Location of children's bed should be compatible with their birthdates.

小孩房的床位，宜命、向相配方論吉。

18. ABOUT THE BED

Aside from the room structure, the arrangement of bed is of great importance. Proper arrangement can ensure occupants of luck and opportunities for advancement. A bed positioned well can connect good ch'i, balance and enhance it's flow to positively affect the occupants' health and ultimate performance at work.

Many people believe that the facing of the bed has certain geomantic implication or influence on the occupant, such as :

North	- helps develop intuition.
Northeast	- helps in work relating to research and experimentation.
East	- sleep will be peaceful.
Southeast	- will have perseverance in work.
South	- will have good reputation.
Southwest	- helps in matter relating to love.
West	- will have good children.
Northwest	- will have many friends.

In actuality, such beliefs have no basis. The birthdate of the occupant or sleeper is of prime consideration in determining the proper facing for good feng shui. The problem, however, is that both husband and wife sleep on the same bed and they have different birthdates. This situation can only be resolved by locating the place with the best ch'i flow for the bed.

Also, many people are unclear or do not know whether geomantic influence applies to the facing of the bed, the facing of the sleeper's head or the facing of the sleeper's feet. Feng shui experts agree that geomantic influence applies to the facing of the sleeper's head.

Enumerated below are the rules on the location of the bed:

1. bed should not be placed under a beam.
2. bed should not face bedroom door.
3. there should be no opening above the bed.
4. bed should not face a mirror.
5. bed should not be located between two posts.
6, bed should not face toilet door.
7. bed should not face a corner.
8. bed should not face a window showing water storage tank or chimney.
9. stove, sink, or water closet seated at the back of the bed's headboard is unfavorable.
10. the bed's headboard must be placed against the wall.

Further guidelines for bed and it's occupants are:

1. bed should have proper measurement.
2. choose an appropriate date for placing the bed.
3. place "Five Lucky Objects" under the bed.
4. it is not advisable to just put anything or hang anything on or above the front of the bed.
5. lamps at the front of the bed should have designs.
6. for newly weds, it is advisable to put an auspicious item at the front of the bed so as to have babies soon,
7. round shaped bed is not advisable.
8. the front of the bed and the bedroom door should not be parallel or along the same line.
9. bed should not be moved when the wife is pregnant.
10. choose an appropriate date for replacing the bed.

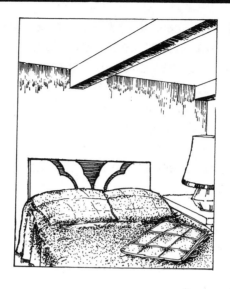

90. Bed under a beam is unfavorable.
床上忌有橫樑。

91. Bed should not face a mirror.
床忌對鏡。

92. The bed facing the bedroom's door is bad.
床忌對門。

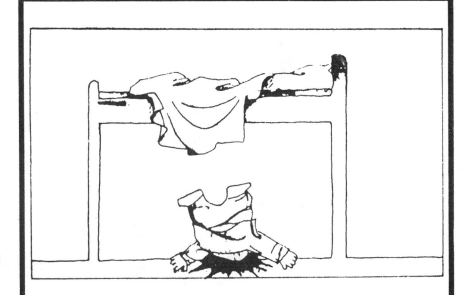

93. Avoid using a bed that is too high.
床忌太高度。

94. Bed located in between two posts is bad.
床忌在柱下。

95. Bed facing the toilet door is bad.
床忌對浴廁門。

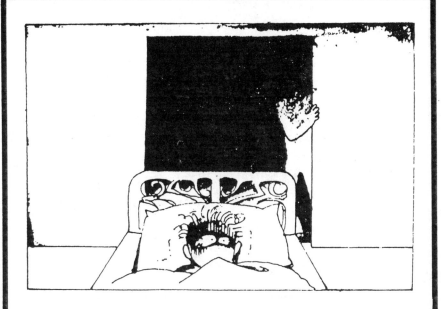

98. The back of the headboard should not be placed in front of a door.
床不可背對門。

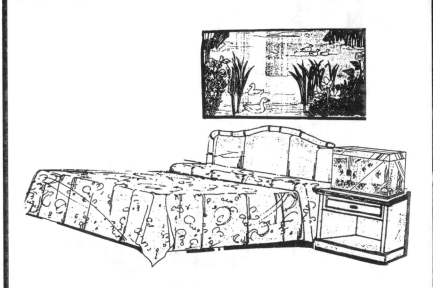

99. Water closet seated at the back of the bed's headboard is unfavorable.
床頭上忌擺魚缸。

100. The bed's headboard that has a window at the back is bad.
床頭忌不靠壁。

101. A hanging cabinet above the headboard is bad.
床頭位上不可設櫃架。

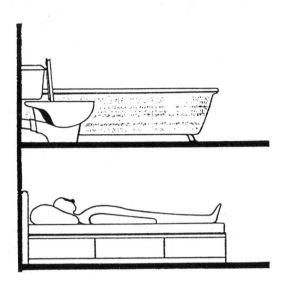

102. The toilet should not be located above the location of the bed.

床上方忌有浴廁。

103. Bed should not be moved when the wife is pregnant.

婦女懷孕時，忌移床。

19.   THE KITCHEN AND THE STOVE

Kitchen is the place where both water and fire are used. Good interaction or balance between these two elements will result in good fortune while adverse interaction will bring about misfortune. A kitchen represents wealth. It is perceive that food feeds a person's health and effectiveness, so that the better the food is, the more capable and healthy the person will be and the larger his potential income will be.

In the kitchen, the most significant appliance that needs feng shui attention is the stove. Symbolically, the stove figures prominently in a home's finances. It should be clean and work smoothly so that money or wealth can easily enter the home. Proper positioning of the kitchen and the stove is indeed very important. If located in a good place, the residents can expect good fortune, otherwise, illness and depletion of money and assets will be the consequences.

It is strongly advised to observe the following pointers regarding the stove's position :
1. stove should not face the main door.
2. stove should not face the toilet door.
3. stove should not face the door of the master bedroom.
4. avoid having big window behind the stove.
5. stove should not be placed above the sewerage or water pipe.
6. stove should not be placed under a beam.
7. stove should not be placed in corners.
8. stove should not be placed in between two faucets.
9. stove should not be located in the middle of the house.
10. stove seated at the back of toilet sink or water closet is not advisable.
11. stove should not face staircase.
12. stove seated at the back of a bed is not good.

Pointers regarding the kitchen are :

TABLE 26

POSITIVE POSITIONS FOR STOVE OR OVEN

1. it should not be located in places where strong wind passes.
2. kitchen should not be located above the septic tank or water storage tank.
3. kitchen should be arranged in such a way that it will be compatible to the fate of the owner. Consult a geomancer on this point.
4. kitchen should not be located in the centerpoint or the lucky spot of the house.
5. it should be provided with good ventilation and lighting.
6. for a 2-storey building, the toilet should not be placed on top of the kitchen.
7. exhaust for the smoke should not be prominently located.
8. waste water pipe line should not pass through sitting room.
9. floor level of the kitchen should be the same as that of the dining room.
10. the roof of the kitchen should not have any opening.
11. the shape of the kitchen should not be round or irregular.
12. place an auspicious object under the platform or table on which the stove is placed.

104. Stove should not be facing the main door.

灶向大門，凶。

105. Stove should not be facing the toilet door.

灶向浴廁門，凶。

106. Stove should not be facing the door of a bedroom.

灶向臥室門，凶。

107. Avoid having big window behind the stove.

灶後有大窗，不吉。

108. Stove should not be placed above the sewerage or water pipe.

灶擺設在水營流經之處的上面，凶。

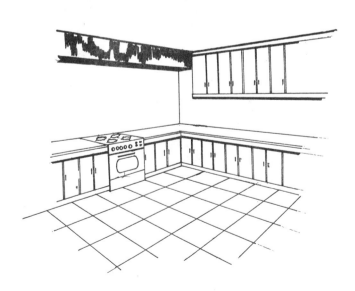

109. Stove should not be placed under a beam.

灶上方忌橫樑壓著。

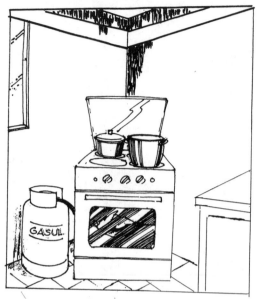

110. Stove should not be placed at the corners.

灶忌擺設在牆壁交角處。

111. Stove should not be placed in between two faucets.

灶在兩水之中間，論凶。

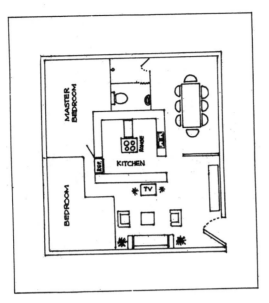

112. Stove should not be placed in the center of the house.

灶在住宅中心點上，凶。

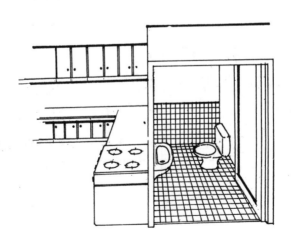

113. Stove seated at the back of a toilet sink is not advisable.

灶後有廁壺、水壺，均凶。

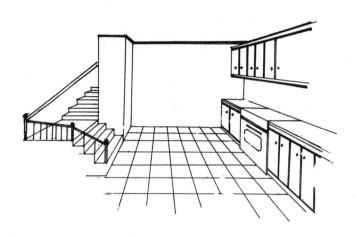

114. Stove should not be facing a staircase.

灶向樓梯，凶。

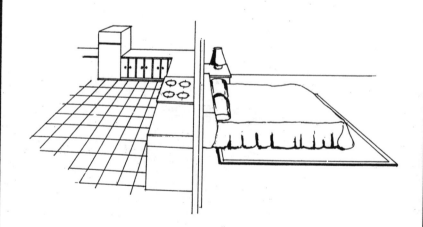

115. Stove seated at the back of a bed is unfavorable.

灶後有床，不吉。

118. It is very auspicious to place "5 lucky objects" under the platform on which the stove is placed.

廚房秘藏「五寶」，大吉大利。

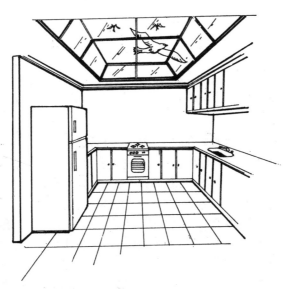

119. The roof of the kitchen should not have any opening.

廚房忌開天窗。

20. ABOUT THE DINING ROOM

Dining room is another one of those parts that need our attention regarding feng shui arrangement. To have a good arrangement for the dining room and its table, the occupants will be sure to have good health.

The key feng shui rules for the dining room are:
1. the dining room should not be near the main door.
2. it should not be located under the staircase.
3. it should not be located on top of the septic tank.
4. the ceiling should not have an opening or window.
5. avoid placing large mirror in the dining room.

For the dining table, observe the following:

1. the auspicious or desirable shapes for the table are -

2. the unlucky or undesirable shapes are -

3. preferred materials for dining table are wood or wood with iron. Avoid tables made of glass or marble.
4. the dining table should not face any door.
5. neither should it face the staircase.
6. ceiling beam above the dining table is not favorable.
7. drainage pipes running along the ceiling above the dining table is not good.
8. dining table should never face the toilet door.

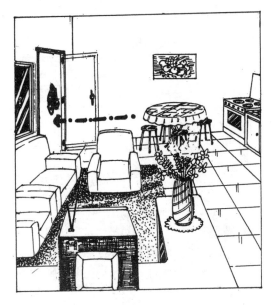

122. A dining room facing the main door is unfavorable.

餐廳忌對著大門。

123. A dining room should not be cluttered with too much things and it should not be dirty.

餐廳忌雜亂無章。

124. The ceiling of a dining room should not have an opening or window.

餐廳忌開天窗。

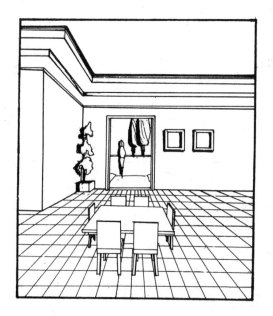

125. A dining table facing the main door is bad.

餐桌忌對著大門或後門。

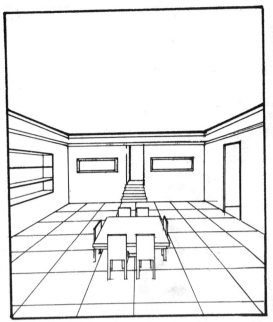

126. A dining table that faces the staircase is unfavorable.
餐桌忌對著樓梯。

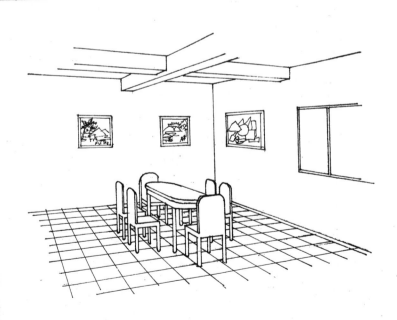

127. A ceiling beam above a dining table is unfavorable.
餐桌忌在橫樑直柱下。

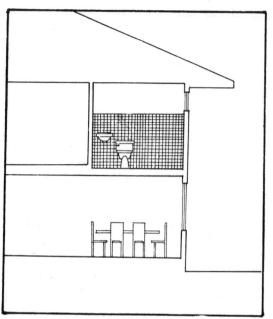

128. A toilet located on top of a dining table is unfavorable.
餐桌忌在浴廁下。

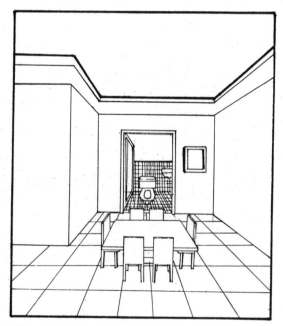

129. A dining table facing the toilet door is bad.
餐桌忌對著廁門。

21. THE TOILET AND THE BATHROOM

Toilet and bathrooms (T & B) are generally considered together and are indicators of one's health and prosperity. Bathroom, the place where water (money) escapes, is a symbol of family members' internal plumbing and expenses. Never place the bathroom on the "lucky spot" of the house or finances will be drained.

The following four locations of the toilet and bathroom are considered unfavorable :

Southwest or Northeast - will adversely affect health.

Center of the house - will lose wealth or money.

Beside or facing the main door - will not be good for reputation.

True South - occupants will be uncooperative.

Generally, these feng shui guidelines are to be observed for the proper location of toilet and bathroom :

1. for 2-storey house, T&B should not be located on top of the main door.
2. it should not be located in places considered lucky for attracting wealth.
3. it should not be visible from the main door.
4. it should not be located beside the main door.
5. it should not be located in prominent places.
6. it should be kept clean.
7. it should have good ventilation.
8. it should be located in places with window and properly lighted.
9. toilet bowl should not be in direct line with the toilet door.
10. T&B should not face a stove.
11. it should not be higher than the rooms' floor level.
12. drainage pipe should not pass through places considered lucky for attracting wealth.

TABLE 27

UNFAVORABLE POSITION OF TOILET AND BATHROOM

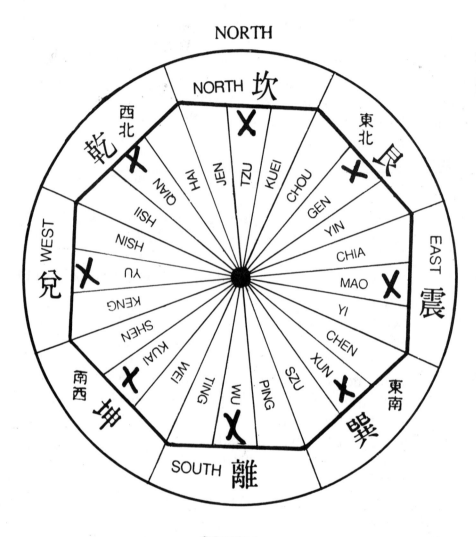

13. it should not face a staircase.
14. it should not face the main door.
15. it should not face the bed in a bedroom.

For bedrooms with connecting toilet and bathroom, the following locations in exact degree readings are considered bad or unfavorable :

30* East - sons and daughters will like to gallivant.

10* Southeast - daughters will have unhappy love affairs. Abdominal problems are indicated.

30* South - will meet accidents such as fire.

30* Southwest - worst location.

10* Northwest - sons and daughters will be argumentative with parents.

10* North - will adversely affect health.

60* Northeast - worst location.

30* West - abdominal problems are indicated.

130. For a 2-storey house, T & B should not be located on the top of the main door.

浴廁設在大門上方，大凶。

131. T & B should not be located beside the main door.

浴廁設在大門左或右傍，均凶。

134. T & B facing a stove is unfavorable.

浴廁對著灶，凶。

135. A toilet door that opens directly to show the toilet bowl is bad.

廁壺對著門，論凶。

22.   THE   STAIRCASE

The staircase of the house is very important since it connects the ch'i upstairs and downstairs. The number of steps in a staircase are considered carefully. Traditionally, the steps are counted in a 3-steps or 4-steps pattern. The 3-steps pattern is the gold - silver - death cycle; while the 4-steps is the good luck-prosperity-bad luck-failure cycle. The last step should be either gold or silver or good luck or prosperity; therefore the good numbers of steps are 1, 2, 5, 10, 13, 14, 17 and 22. Location of staircase:

A feng shui expert or geomancer can determine the best location for your staircase by using the Chinese compass. Generally, the following orientations can enhance either good ch'i or bad ch'i regarding the fate, fortune and status of the owner. If the places has . . . . .

Life-force ch'i - the owner's fate will surely improve.

Lucky ch'i - will gradually improve.

Smooth ch'i - luck will be variable.

Fluctuating ch'i - luck will slowly deteriorate.

Unlucky ch'i - luck will vary significantly.

Evil ch'i - will suffer much because family member or members will commit wrong or shameful acts and reputation will be destroyed.

Suffocating ch'i - will gradually deteriorate because of money matters and illness in family.

Six major points regarding staircase:

1. staircase should not face the main door.
2. staircase should not be located in the middle of the house.
3. staircase should not face toilet door.
4. staircase should not face bedroom door.
5. staircase should not be in the direction of a fence corner.

6. do not have two staircase facing each other.

Other pointers are :

1. staircase should not be too steep, narrow nor should it have many curves or turns, or spiral.
2. a landing with a short turn at the middle of a staircase is good.
3. stove should not be placed under the staircase neither should it face the staircase.
4. there should be good lighting along the staircase.
5. to attract good ch'i and bring good luck to the owner, it is important that during the construction of the staircase, remember to place or bury five lucky objects in each step of a concrete staircase or have the five lucky objects in the first and last steps of a wooden staircase.

136. Stove placed under the staircase is unfavorable.

梯下忌設灶。

137. Staircase too steep or narrow is bad.

梯忌太窄太陡。

138. Staircase facing a toilet is bad.

梯忌對浴廁門。

139. Staircase facing the main door is unfavorable.

梯忌對大門。

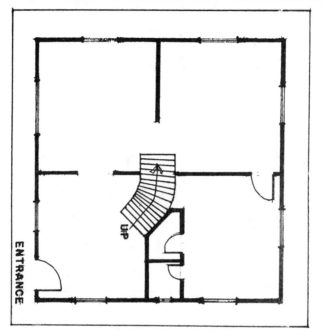

140. Staircase located in the middle of the house is bad.

梯忌設在住宅中心點上。

141. Two staircase facing each other in a house is unfavorable.

住宅中設有兩個樓梯對走，凶。

142. Staircase facing the direction of a fence corner is bad.

梯忌對著房角。

143. Staircase facing the bedroom is bad.

梯忌對著臥室之門。

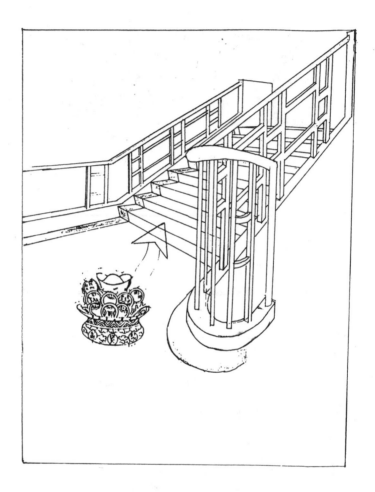

144. It is auspicious to place "5 - lucky objects" in each step of the staircase during the construction.

梯階藏「五寶」，能招財引福。

23.   ON THE ALTAR

The altar is the most sacred place in the house. It is most lucky and prosperous for the owner to have the altar located in the most favorable orientation related to him. Always keep the altar clean and lighted. To have a pair of vigil light on the altar is advisable.

When setting up an altar at home, one should observe the following pointers :

1. images of Saints made of tiles should not be formed from more than one tile.
2. images of Saints that are made of wood should be solid and not hollow.
3. the facial features of Saints made from bronze material should be pronounced.
4. the pictures of Saints should be looking downward.
5. consult a priest or minister regarding any damages on the images of Saints.

For the altar table, these will apply :

1. table made of wood or concrete is preferable.
2. table made of iron should not be incompatible with the element of the house.
3. table made of glass is unfavorable.
4. table should have proper dimension.
5. scissors, medicines and unclean objects should not be placed on the altar.

For the location of the altar, these guidelines should be considered :

1. altar should not be located under the staircase or near the toilet.

2. there should be no toilet at the backside or beside the altar.
3. the altar should not face the door of a toilet or sink.
4. altar should not face any corner of the house.
5. altar should not face a post or placed under a beam.

Additional recommendations regarding the altar are :

1. the urn for joss sticks should be made of brass and not marble.
2. the height of the urn should not exceed the height of Buddha or Saint's stomach.
3. place "Five Lucky Objects" in the urn.
4. any lighting above the head of the Buddha or Saint should be circular in shape.
5. candles or lamps for the altar should be in pair and of the same design.
6. request the minister to bless the statues and the altar.
7. consult the minister on the date and time before setting up the altar.
8. the appropriate offerings at the altar are fresh flowers, tea, fruits, sweets like candies.
9. house displaying pictures of ancestors should have an altar for Buddha or Saints.
10. light candles or offer incense by burning joss sticks every morning.

145. Avoid locating the altar under a staircase.

神案忌設在梯下。

146. Avoid locating the altar at the backside of the toilet.

神案忌設在浴廁牆壁後面。

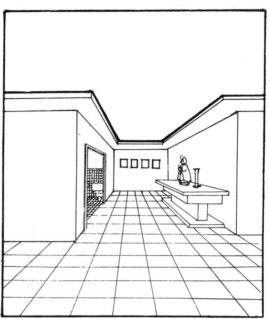

147.　An altar facing the toilet is bad.
神案忌對著浴廁。

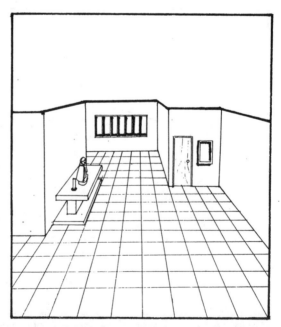

148.　An altar should not face the corner of the room.
神案忌對著房間尖角。

24. SWIMMING POOL AND GARDEN

This section introduces the essential feng shui guides regarding garden and swimming pool. As an added part of the residence, it is advisable to coordinate the ch'i of these places to the other parts of the house. Remember the following :

1. it is most important to locate the swimming pool in a good place; consult a geomancer.
2. swimming pool must always be filled with water, preferably filtered and clean.
3. swimming pool located at the west side can bring bad luck.
4. rectangular pool or one with many corners is unfavorable.
5. pool should never be located in the center of the house.
6. pool should not be located in a high place.
7. drainage located at each end of the pool is not advisable.
8. the design for grotto or fountain should not have many corners.
9. avoid designing grotto with three structures pointed upwards.
10. the statue of Saints should not face house corner or a post.
11. the grotto should always be lighted.
12. dead flowers along the grotto should be replaced and repair should be done for damages on the fountain.
13. avoid using crazy cut tiles in the garden.
14. the garden should not have rocks that resemble animals.
15. a big tree inside the house is unfavorable.
16. dead trees in the garden should be removed.
17. avoid thorny plants or trees in the garden.
18. to balance the ch'i, bury "Five Lucky Objects" in the grotto and pool area.
19. water from pool should not be drained into the septic tank.
20. the roof of the shed or hut in the garden should not have too many corners.
21. select a lucky date for construction of grotto or swimming pool

150. Location of a swimming pool must be considered carefully because it has effects on the health and wealth of the family.

游泳池的方位最關一家人健康財運，必須小心推鑑。

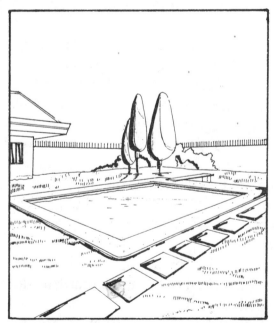

151. A swimming pool must always be filled with water.

泳池之水宜常保持八分滿，方論吉。

152. A swimming pool with many corners is unfavorable.
泳池奇形或多角均不吉。

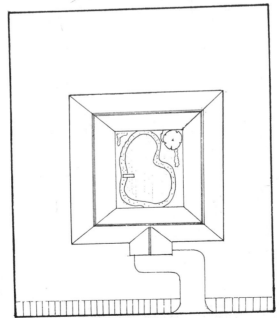

153. A swimming pool located at the center of the house is unfavorable.
泳池設在宅地中心大凶。

154. A garden should not have rocks that resembles animals.

花園忌擺置奇形怪狀石塊。

155. The statue of saints should not face the corner of the house or post.

假山神位忌對尖角。

25.   THE   OFFICE

Everyone aspires to be successful in business or career undertakings. Having fame and power are dreams we aspire to reach. But we tend to blame our fate for the failure of our aspirations. This is not the right way to think about failure.

Although fate has something to do with our life, you will be surprised to know that there are ways to alter fate and avert misfortunes. One solution that can generate luck and success is through feng shui. Good feng shui can entice the good ch'i of the place and eventually help business prosper and foster pleasant and harmonious relationships among management and staff.

Thus, consider the following rules :

1. consult an expert on the most favorable location that will suit you.
2. rectangular or square type of room is good. Avoid irregular shapes such as areas with three corners, with missing corner or "L" type of place.
3. do not locate your office on dead-end road.
4. be sure to arrange the furnitures like the table and chairs in harmonious relation with the ch'i of the place.
5. use talisman like "the **Lucky-8-Treasures®**" to enhance luck.
6. arrange plants inside offices and have them in lucky places.
7. if you are to display flower vases, choose the colors suited to you and consider the best location for each.
8. display of aquarium needs lucky places, too. Some individuals are not suited to have aquarium in their office.
9. do not have window on the office ceiling.
10. display only appropriate paintings or verses on your office walls.
11. avoid having multi-edge design on your ceiling.
12. keep electrical, telephone wires and airducts out of sight.
13. avoid having big beams and posts inside the office.
14. do not locate the comfort rooms near the entrance of the office.
15. the offices of the treasury, finance and accounting should avoid having mirror at the back and sides of the table.

1. Consult an expert on the most favorable position that will suit you.

   辦公室的門位，要能招財納福。

2. Irregular shapes of office is unfavorable.

   辦公室忌缺角。

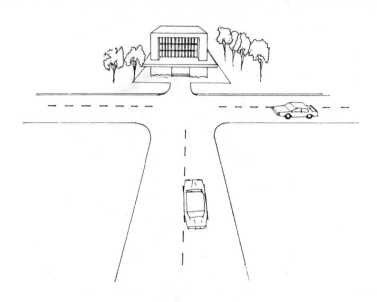

3. Don't locate your office at the end of a dead road.

   辦公室忌路沖。

4. Be sure to arrange the tables, chairs and furnitures in harmonious relation within the ch'i of the place.

   辦公室的桌椅擺設，忌擋阻財路。

5. Use talisman like the "Lucky 8 Treasures®" to enhance luck.

辦公室懸掛「八寶靈卦」＊，財運亨通。

6. Arrange plants inside offices in lucky places.

辦公室盆景須擇方位。

7. To display flower vases, choose the colors suited to you and consider the best location for each.

不同方位，盆景顏色須相生配方吉。

8. Display of aquarium needs lucky places too. Some persons are not suited to have aquarium displayed in their offices.

魚缸位置最關係財源。

9. Do not locate windows on the ceiling of your office

辦公室忌開天窗。

10. Display only appropriate paintings or verses on your office walls.

辦公室的壁畫，忌任意安裝。

11. Avoid multi-edges design on your ceiling.

辦公室天花板忌凸凹角度過多。

12. Keep electrical, telephone wires and airducts out of sight.

通風排氣管、電線電纜宜隱藏。

13. Avoid having big beams and posts inside the office.

辦公室忌有橫樑或柱明顯突出。

14. Do not locate comfort rooms near the entrance of the office.

辦公室忌入門就看到廁所。

15. Avoid placing mirror in the office of treasury, finance and accounting.

財務會計部忌有大鏡。

26. OFFICE TABLE

As important as the feng shui of an office is the proper arrangement of tables and chairs including other office furnitures. Following are the do's and don'ts of office table arrangement :

1. tables should be in parallel arrangement.
2. the owner's table or that of the highest ranking officer should be located in the most lucky place.
3. the chief officer's table should be located in a place wherein mobility is not possible behind him.
4. display talisman on top of the table, such as the Holy Gourd.®″
5. inquire about the most favorable measurement of the table.
6. it is helpful to display "the Lucky-8-Treasures®" on the table of the Finance officer.
7. do not display obscure objects on top of the table, such as snake, horns.
8. the table should not be placed directly in front of the door.
9. do not have a door situated at the back of your place, too.
10. tables should not be located on curving corners of the room.
11. avoid having an exposed beam above the table.
12. do not place the table in front of toilet.
13. do not have a glass window at the backside of your place.
14. do not place the table beside a post, neither is it good to have the post in front of the table.
15. never place the table in front of a pointed object or the corner of a room's partition.
16. do not place the table under a staircase.
17. the manager sitting with his/her back against solid wall is favorable.
18. the vault facing the door is unfavorable.

1. Tables should be in parallel arrangement.
   辦公桌的方位要正。

2. The owner's table or that of the higher ranking officer should be located in the most lucky place.
   老闆的辦公桌方位須配合生辰八字。
   老闆的辦公桌在財位上最吉。

3. Mobility behind the chief officer's table should be avoided.
    老闆的辦公桌後方忌有人走動。

4. Display talisman like "Holy Gourd®" on top of the table.
    辦公桌上夾有「生財葫蘆」＊大吉利。

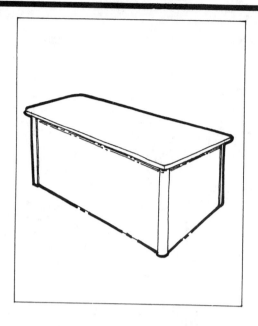

5. Inquire about the most favorable measurement of the table.

辦公桌要有一定呎吋。

6. It is helpful to display the ”**Lucky-8-Treasures**®”

財政桌位，懸掛「八寶靈卦」＊，必有意想不到的利益

7. Do not display obscure or odd objects on top of the table.
　辦公桌上忌擺猛獸裝飾品。

8. Table should not be placed directly in front of the door.
　辦公桌忌對著門。

9. Do not locate a door at the back of your table.

    辦公桌忌背門坐。

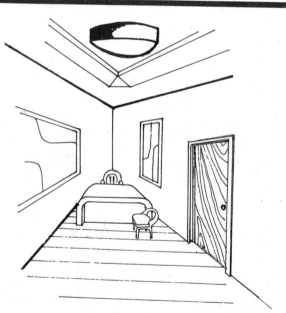

10. Table should not be located at the curving corners of the room.

    辦公桌位忌處彎角。

11. Avoid having an exposed beam above the table.
忌有橫樑壓辦公桌。

12. Do not locate the table in front of a toilet
桌忌對廁所。

13. Do not install glass windows at the backside of your place.
    辦公桌背後忌有落地窗。

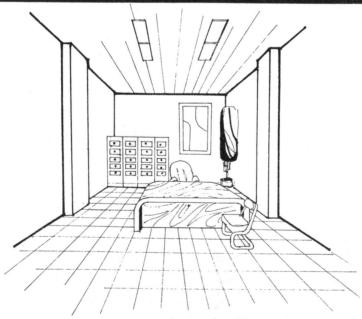

14. Do not place the table beside a post, neither it is good to have the post infront of the table.
    左右大柱夾桌，大忌。

15. Never place a table in front of a pointed object or at the corner of a room's partition

辦公桌忌對尖角。

27. AQUARIUM

People like to have an aquarium in the house mainly for aesthetic reason. However, it is advisable to know the feng shui implications about aquarium before deciding where to place one in the house.

A brief background information regarding the "five elements" is relevant for a better understanding and appreciation of this subject.
The Chinese hope to improve their ch'i and fate by examining their five elements. Out of the interplay of yin and yang come five manifestations of ch'i: wood, earth, fire, water and metal. Like yin, yang and ch'i, the five elements are not physical substances but powers or essences describing all matters and attributes.

The five elements have relative effects on each other, creating and destroying one another in fixed succession. The cycle of development goes like this : fire produces earth (ash); earth produces metal (minerals); metal creates water (although water rusts metal.This order derives from the observation that when water is in a metal cup, water forms on the outside of the vessel); water feeds wood (trees need water to grow); and wood aids fire. The chain of destruction is : wood harms earth ; earth obstructs water ; water destroys fire; fire melts metal ; and metal chops down wood.

Human ch'i can also be divided into wood, earth, metal, water and fire. Everyone has the five elements in varying amounts,i.e., one can have a lot or a little of an element although the ideal state is to have a balanced amount of each element. A geomancer can determine the amount of each element in a person.

Generally, it is not advisable for a person with fire element to own an aquarium (which is represented by water) because water and fire are in opposition or are in the destructive cycle (water destroys fire). However, a person with too much fire element may own a small aquarium to counter the excess amount of the fire element. Likewise, a person who lacks the water element may want to own an aquarium while one with a lot of the water element already should not own an aquarium. The general idea is to achieve a balanced amount of the element,i.e., neither too much nor too little or reduce if too much and add if too little.

Six feng shui guidelines regarding the aquarium are as follows :

1. a person should first consult a geomancer regarding his elements and their corresponding amounts before owning an aquarium.

2. the best location for an aquarium is generally in the east, southeast portion of the house. It is advisable for persons with the elements listed below to follow the suggested location of the aquarium and the suggested color for the aquarium stand.

   wood - north and green color.
   earth - southwest and light blue color.
   metal - north and white color.
   water - north or east and white or green color.
   fire - generally not advised to own an aquarium.

3. the best shape for the aquarium is either rectangular or round. However, the ones associated to elements are :

round	metal	good
hexagonal	water	okey
square	earth	avoid
rectangular	wood	okey
triangular	fire	avoid

4. the quantity of fishes in an aquarium should be 1, 4, 6 or 9. Sizes are not relevant but the number relative to the five elements are :

water -	1,	6	fire - 2,	7
wood -	3,	8	metal - 4,	9
earth -	5,	10		

5. decorations used for aquarium should simulate its natural setting like the plants and rocks. Do not put odd or unusual objects inside the aquarium.

6. a) to prevent loss of wealth, aquarium should not be located in any bedroom.

b) if an aquarium was located in the study room, it should not be placed in a spot which will affect the mind of the children; otherwise, the implication is that the children will be mischievous and will not like to study.

c) an aquarium placed in the kitchen will adversely affect pregnancy.

d) generally, an aquarium is placed in the living or sitting room. However, it should not be placed on the love spot facing the outside of the house. Otherwise, husband or other members of the family may engage in illicit love affairs.

28.   WIND CHIMES

Those tiny bells strung together and hanged on doors, windows and living rooms are the usual feature of wind chimes we use in our homes. The tingling sound of the bells can sooth and ease unpleasant feelings. It can forewarn occupant of other person's presence. In feng shui, these chimes are generally used as moderators of ch'i flow. They can disperse malign interior and exterior ch'i by tempering and redirecting ch'i for a more beneficial, balanced way.

Chimes or bells can be used to summon positive ch'i and money into a home or business. Hanging them on eaves will symbolically raise a house ch'i. Placing them in the living room can help harmonize the ch'i and elements of the place. Like all other decorations however, putting up chimes must also be done with care to be certain of their effectiveness. Here are some pointers for your guide :

1. you should know whether you need to have a wind chime or not.
2. find out from the geomancer where to locate the "ngo-hong and the dee-o" places in your home. These places have the evil or dead ch'i, therefore, these should be corrected or changed by hanging chimes on the place.
3. it is better to use chimes that are blessed.
4. choose the proper date of putting the chimes up.
5. the chimes used for feng shui purposes are those with bronze material in the middle. Usually, the bronze item has words or pictures inscribed on it.
6. choose the color of the chimes. Use the color compatible to your element. Multi-colored bells are nice to look at but they are not very effective and can be counter - productive sometime.

29. OTHER INTERIOR DECORATIONS

Nowadays, it is common to find houses using plants, vases, toys, antique items and even stuff animals as decorations or accents at home. These items can have influence on a person's behavioural patterns and life course. To ensure attainment of positive and healthy ch'i, below are some basic guidelines to be observed:

1. floor plants - choose fresh plants with rounded leaves and preferably green color. Avoid plants with thorns.

2. hanging plants - this should not be placed in the master bedroom.

3. piano - place this on the dragon side.

4. sword - this should not be displayed in children's or study room.

5. stuffed wild animals - these are not advisable for bedrooms.

6. jars and big vases - choose the appropriate location for these items; be sure to move these things from time to time.

7. big anahaw fan - this should not be placed in front of door entrance.

8. dolls and stuffed toys - unused toys especially those broken, torn, or tattered should not be kept inside the room.

9. antiques - it is advisable to know the origin of these items; suggested location for each kind are as follows:
   a. made of stone - place this on the southwest or northeast side of the house.

b. made of porcelain - on the north side.

c. made of wood - on southeast or east.

d. made of metal - on west or northwest.

10. pictures or paintings - pictures about water should not be placed in bedroom or above headboard. Too many birds in a painting should not be displayed in the dining room.

11. lion - it is best to display lions in pair and have their heads facing the door.

12. tiger - this kind should be in lying position with it's head facing away from the door.

13. horse - display this in six or eight pieces and have their heads facing the house.

14. goat - this should be in three pieces placed together.

15. rooster - it is best to display this kind in the garden, never in bedrooms.

16. dragon - it should be placed in living room or study room.

17. carabao - it should be in two pieces, one big and the other small.

18. dog - it should be displayed with head facing the door.

30.   METHODS OF ASSESSING FENG SHUI

There are basically two methods of assessing and solving feng shui problems for a site or an interior. These are the LUO-PAN-TING KENG and the HSUAN-CHIH-LING - FA.

The Luo-pan-ting-keng is the logical , rational way. This method makes use of the luo-pan or Chinese compass. A luo-pan is used to determine the flow of ch'i and the orientation of buildings, rooms and furniture. The various rings of the luo-pan are designed according to directional and cosmological systems. The eight trigrams, the twelve branches, twenty eight constellations of Chinese astrology, the ten stems and the eight favorable and unfavorable star signs of destiny are all incorporated in the luo-pan. Usually in the luo-pan-ting-keng method, the solution on designs and placement or arrangement of objects are reasonable and we can easily grasp the idea based on our own experience and knowledge.

The Hsuan -chih -ling -fa is more complicated in a way, because it is illogical and sometimes mystical. The solution depends largely on the physical features or topographical characteristics of the land. The intuitive approach includes the great expanse outside our known world and within our subconscious. Four general techniques in this method are :

HSUAN-CHIH-LING - FA.

LUO- PAN-TING KENG

1. channeling ch'i - this taps or makes use of ch'i that is either too far or too deep beneath the earth. To do this, bury "**Five Lucky Objects**" in the ground to lift the ch'i from the earth; or put the "**Five Lucky Objects**" inside the beam of the house to attract atmospheric ch'i .

2. balancing ch'i - the places commonly used by the residents such as gates, main door, back door, living and dining rooms are very important. To ensure equilibrium of ch'i for the house, it is advisable to put "**Five Lucky Objects**" on each of the places mentioned.

3. enhancing ch'i - to enhance could mean either to increase or to modify the flow of ch'i. The usage of colors that are compatible to the elements of the house and its occupants can churn up weak ch'i; while placement of an auspicious item like the "**Lucky-8-Treasures®**" on the "lucky spot" inside the house can activate stagnant ch'i and help it circulate through the house.

4. transforming bad ch'i - dangerous ch'i like that which can suffocate or ch'i of evil force should be corrected. The balance between yin and yang ch'i must be attain to help in this method. Example: if the evil ch'i is from the outside, the corners of the house must have auspicious items buried in each part of the house. On the other hand, the suffocating ch'i can be corrected by placing special objects or amulets inside the center part of the house. This is done to enhance the good ch'i of the place and have it counteract the suffocating effect of the bad ch'i.

   At present, geomancers tend to combine the two methods in their practice but they consider the hsuan-chih-ling-fa assessment as of prime importance because of its deeper analysis of the situation. The special objects mentioned herein should be properly blessed. Sometimes, it is necessary for the Minister to personally perform the rituals needed for more effectivity.

31. CONSTRUCTION AND RENOVATION

In any construction, the foundation or the base should be taken cared of diligently. Some people tend to pay more attention to the house's architectural design or it's interior decorations; not fully understanding the probable losses they may incur if the foundation for the building or house is weak.

When planning to build your house, consider these eight pointers before construction :

1. know the kind of soil you have. Is it solid, sandy, muddy or rocky ? Ask your engineer about this matter.
2. avoid the following conditions for residential sites, because these are unlucky :
   a) if the place was formerly a funeral parlor or a cemetery.
   b) if murder took place on the site.
   c) if the site was formerly a garbage dumpsite or garbage was burned there.
   d) a big fire had occured on the site.
   e) the place has several big, old trees.
3. observe the area's vicinity. Know the important facts like the zoning of the locality, the roads and the trail of sewers. Study the plots and shapes of the neighboring houses.
4. when getting rid of the plants grown on the lot, be sure to abate the roots of the trees totally.
5. consult a geomancer on the kind of structure that will be most favorable to you. For the owner to be lucky, it is best that the position of the rooms and other essential parts of the house be complimentary to each other.
6. ask the geomancer for the time when it is best to begin the construction work.
7. during construction, when the foundation for the posts and other essential parts of the house are to be done, remember to include "Five Lucky Objects" in each diggings. This is done to enhance the good feng shui of the place.

8. lastly, to attain smooth flow of work and good ch'i for the place, avoid any quarrels or entanglements with workers during construction.

Renovation is almost as tedious as construction. Major repairs can cost a lot and it can alter the condition and the flow of the place's ch'i. So that one can be sure that things are done correctly and for the benefit of the owner, he has to . . . . .

1. make sure that the year or the time of undertaking the renovation will not be counterproductive to the owner of the house. Simply said, choose the best time and day for renovation.

2. take care not to destroy the good ch'i of the site when renovation is being done.

3. renovation should be deferred when there is a pregnant woman in the house.

4. broken pipeline or any water connections must be fixed immediately. When there are dead canals or dried up water passages, put filling materials on it and build a new water passage instead.

5. in case of doubts, consult a feng shui expert.

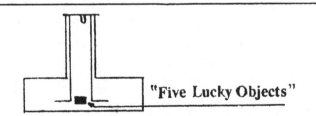

"Five Lucky Objects"

DURING construction, when foundation for posts and other essential parts of the house are being done, put 5 lucky objects in each digging. This will enhance the good Feng Shui of the place. This practice is being done even in prosperous and well-developed countries such as Japan and Singapore.

In case you want to know more about the details of the procedural process and the 5 lucky objects; or you have already built your house and would want to put the lucky objects to improve the condition of your place, consult REV. WONG SENGTIAN at SHENG LIAN Temple.

32. WHEN MOVING TO A NEW PLACE

To have a place of our own is always a joy to us. At the same time we wish to be lucky, prosperous and happy while living in it. Here are some pointers to help ensure your house will be properly attuned to favorable forces of Mother Nature :

1. before moving to a new place, inspect the electrical and waterways of the house. Clean the place.
2. list down all the birthdates of the members of the family and people to live in the house. Consult the feng shui expert on how to arrange the position of the beds. Arrangement of bed is important because each member has his/her own suitable corner.
3. be sure to put a talisman on the main door and the back door of the house. This object will ensure that evil spirits will not join you in moving in.
4. choose a lucky date for moving in.
5. upon moving, it is always best to bring in the statue of Saints first, followed by your money, rice, oil, sugar, and salt before anything else. The couple should move in together.
6. Pregnant women should not join in moving to a new place. It is advisable to have them give birth first before transferring to a new house. In case moving is so urgent and could not be postponed, consult a feng shui expert and ask him for some way to counter the ill effects that might happen.
7. once you have moved in, operate all your appliances, switch on the lights, open the faucets. This is to be sure that things are in order.
8. in earlier years, it was customary to have fireworks when moving to a new place, but since this is seldom practiced now, you can have music played instead; and have your new place blessed by a priest or minister.

9. on the first day of living in your new house, be sure to drink the water of the place. This is to signify your acceptance of the conditions of the place.
10. to complete the process of moving, be sure to sleep- in the first night. In case you can not do so, have a complete set of night clothing, placed neatly on the bed.

SUPER TALISMAN
HOLY LOTUS ®

3. Be sure to put a talisman on the maindoor and the backdoor of the house. This object will ensure that evil spirits will not join you in moving in.

33. FENG SHUI ABOUT LOVE

Most people believe that after their wedding day, their future lives are assured of mutual well-being and happiness. Facts, however, state that less than half of married couples fail to realize the common phrase attached to weddings:"... and they lived happily forever after."

The success of any marriage never comes automatically. Couples must work for it. There will come times of challenge; there will be difficulties and problems. Marriage, like any other human experience calls for inner strength and greater restraints. Feng shui in a way can help ease problems and help love grow, nurture, heal, liberate and unite couples. Here are some important tips :

1. a master's bedroom without any window is not good for marital relation.
2. improper placement of decorative plants can adversely affect the marital relation.
3. erroneous location of aquarium display is to be avoided.
4. do not use decorative stones with irregular shapes or mysterious features in the living room.
5. bedroom with irregular shape should not be used by newly wed couples.

6. a room with too many corners is not good.
7. a tri-angular bedroom is not good.
8. do not place the bed underneath an exposed beam.
9. do not place the bed in between two posts.
10. do not put window above the bed.
11. do not place the bed facing the toilet.
12. do not place the dressing table with its mirror opposite the bed; this is to avoid impairments to your health.
13. place 5 lucky objects underneath the newly wed's bed to make the relationship lucky.
14. newly wed's bedroom should not be fronting a knife-like road.
15. the ceiling of the room should not have many edges for its design.
16. dark color paints or wallpaper is not good for bedrooms.
17. newly wed's bedroom should not be placed directly above the garage.
18. the doors of your sons and daughters' bedrooms should not be directly opposite to each other.
19. do not have a post in the living room. The bigger the post, the worst effect it has.
20. display of the **Lucky-8-Treasures**® in the living room will bring luck and fortune.
21. stove should not be placed in front of the kitchen sink.
22. unequal sizes of door panels is not good.
23. pictures relating to water scenery when placed above the headboard is unfavorable.
24. Chinese ba-gua should not be used as a design for the master bedroom's ceiling.
25. replace the broken mirror of the dresser.
26. do not have too many slanting eaves for the house.
27. the back of the headboard should not be placed in front of a window.

1. A master's bedroom without any window is not good for marital relations.

   沒有窗子的睡房沒有戀愛。

2. Improper placement of decorative plants inside the house can adversely affect marital relation.

   擺設盆栽須合五行，方有良緣。

3. Erroneous location of aquarium display is not good for marital relation.

魚缸排錯方位，影響子女婚姻。

4. Do not use decorative stones with irregular shapes or mysterious features in the living room.

院中近門奇石重疊，阻礙緣份。

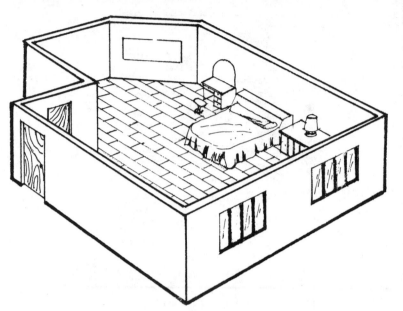

5. Irregular shaped bedroom should not be used by newly-wed couples.

缺角房間不可用做新婚夫妻之房。

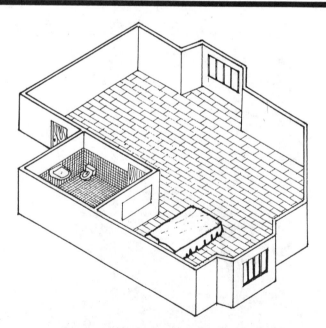

6. A room with too many corners is not good.

多角房間必有感情煩惱。

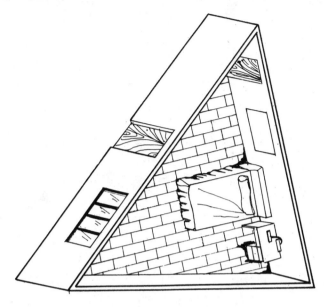

7. A triangular room is not good.

三角形睡房影響性格。

8. Do not place the bed underneath an exposed beam.

橫樑壓床夫妻多口舌。

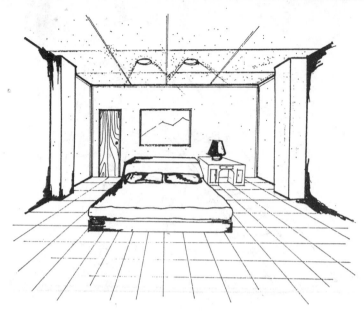

9. Do not place the bed in between two posts.

大柱夾床夫妻難偕白首。

10. Do not put window above the bed.

睡房開天窗，影響健康。

11. The bed should not be facing the toilet.

床對廁所門，身弱多病。

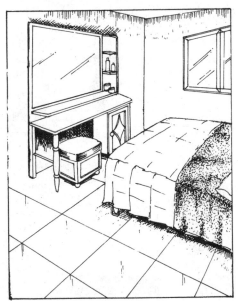

12. Do not place the dressing table at the foot of the bed to avoid health problems.

梳妝鏡台對床不吉祥。

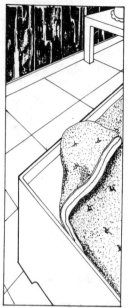

13. Place five lucky objects underneath the bed to make marital relation lucky.

新婚夫妻床底藏「生財葫蘆」＊，大吉大利。

14. Newly-wed's bedroom should not be fronting a knife-like road.

房間路沖，妻財子祿有損。

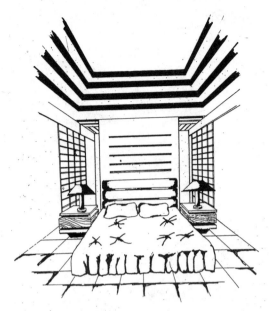

15. The ceiling of the room should not have many edges as a design.

天花板凸凹角度過多，好事多磨。

16. Dark color paints or wallpaper is not good for bedrooms.

牆壁顏色寒黑，婚姻不利。

17. Newly-wed's bedroom should not be directly above the garage.

車庫上面不可用作新婚夫妻睡房。

18. The doors of your sons and daughter's bedrooms should not be directly opposite to each other.

子女睡房房門相對有礙婚姻。

19. Do not locate a post at the living room.

房有獨立大柱，大凶。

20. Unequal sizes of door panels is not good.

門扇左右一大一小，必惹婚外情。

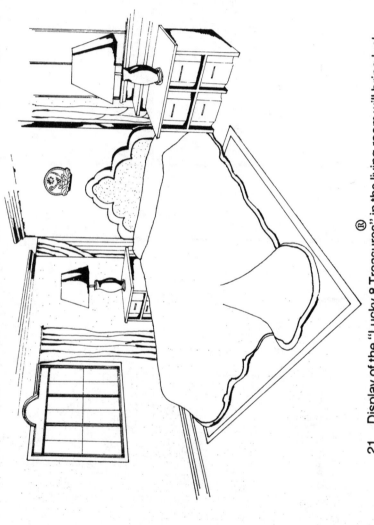

21. Display of the "Lucky 8 Treasures" in the living room will bring luck and fortune.
廳中有「八寶」＊，夫妻和合，婚姻幸福。

22. Stove should not be placed in front of the kitchen sink.

    灶和水相對，情海翻波。

23. Pictures relating to water scenery when placed above the headboard is unfavorable.

    有關流水圖畫，忌掛於床頭壁上。

24. Chinese BA-GUA sign should not be used as a design for ceiling in the master's bedroom.

睡房之天花板，最忌八卦形。

25. Replace the broken mirror of the dresser.

破裂之鏡，不可置於房間。

26. Do not have too slanting eaves for the house.
    屋簷傾斜，忌作睡房。

27. The back of the headboard should not be placed in front of a window.
    床後有大窗，易犯小人。

34.   GHOSTS

Ghost is generally defined as the spirit of a dead person appearing to a living person. Ghosts do exist and are usually hidden in many forms. They may be existing in one's place of work or in one's own house. They can not be avoided, but they can be expelled.

When the magnetic needle of the geomancer's compass keeps moving to the left or right without stopping or it can not steadily point to the north or south direction, then a ghost is suspected to be present within the property or house.

Like everyone, a ghost used to have a living yang or magnetic aura, or ch'i, prior to it's death; which turn the yang into yin ch'i. The yin ch'i of a person who died in an accident or imputation can hold on to a place for a long time because of hatred. A ghost can exist in a land which was previously occupied by a temple, church, hospital, cemetery or which was a place of execution or massacre.

Ghosts can enter a place through several means, such as, attaching itself to a house occupant who had recently attended a funeral service, being attracted by the bad ch'i of the house or through a curse.

The yin ch'i of a ghost will disturb the ch'i of the house. This is similar to the situation of a house ch'i being disturbed by external factors such as being located in a dead-end or T-shaped road, it's door facing a big tree or an electric post. A highly disturbed house ch'i will bring about various problems like unexplained illness, sudden change of temper and mood of the occupants or there might be strange happenings.

The shelter of a ghost can be everywhere; in cabinet, portrait at the living room, in toilet, in picture of animal, on the tree in the the garden or even among the stones. An exorcists or a geomancer gifted with special powers can expel ghosts. Use of amulets can repel entry of ghosts in a place.

Before buying a piece of land or house, it is best to know it's background to avoid future problems or misfortunes.

Part VII : FENG SHUI CURES

After dealing with the topic regarding feng shui on the proper arrangement of furnitures and appliances to favor luck and prosperity, let me discuss some commonly used items to avoid misfortunes, divert mishaps and drive away evil spirits. These items are placed inside the house, at the gate or on the doors.

Generally, we can divide these items into two groups : the first group are things that are used solely as cures while the second group are things that can counteract bad fate and also maintain and enhance the current good fortune that the owner may presently enjoy.

35. FIVE LUCKY OBJECTS

During the olden days, the emperors and royal families of China and Japan practice the ritual of burying "Five Lucky Objects" when they built palaces and mansions for themselves. They would become very successful, lucky, powerful and prosperous and would keep this ritual secretly to themselves. Only until the moment of their deaths would they passed on this secret to their descendants. However, in some instances, the secret was not passed on to the descendants and thus, these families ceased practising this ritual.

Rev. WongSengTian will now reveal this secret about the "Five Lucky Objects" which can not be obtained by any amount of money. The Reverend would like to teach this secret so that everyone will be lucky and prosperous. The teacher of the Reverend's mentor has already helped numerous people in Taiwan, HongKong, and Singapore. They became successful and prosperous. If one is already lucky, he will be even luckier and if one is unlucky, his bad luck will soon pass away.

There are five benefits attributed to these "Five Luck Objects", as follows :

1. they influence and enhance the good ch'i of the house.
2. the ch'i sometimes moves fast, sometimes it moves slowly, sometimes it stops and sometimes it is scattered. The five lucky objects will bring about a smooth movement of the ch'i for tranquility, luck and prosperity.
3. the ch'i will emit some kind of light to drive away evil spirits.
4. the ch'i will neutralize one's bad luck and bring fortune and success.
5. the longer the five lucky objects are buried or kept, the stronger is the good influence.

36. MIRROR

In feng shui, the mirror is a means used to drive away bad luck and correct defects on the size of an area. However, one has to be knowledgeable about the mirror's specific size and shape to attain best results. A lucky date should be determined as to when to put up or install the mirror. Check the mirror's condition if it is cracked or broken. A broken mirror can not counter bad fate and instead, undertakings will not be accomplished or fulfilled.

37. BA - GUA

An octagon shaped amulet divided into eight sections, commonly used as a guide to interpret a person's life, as well as problems and provides a cure to solve them. It can also drive away evil spirits and avert misfortunes. This device is laid on gates or main doors.

Commercially, a ba-gua is available in department stores, ordinarily made of wood, with or without glass in the center. Individuals are forewarned in the idle use of this because wrong positioning of ba-gua may attract bad luck instead of good.

Remember these three important points :

1. consult a feng shui expert for a lucky date or time, to put up the ba-gua.
2. ask the expert where and how to position it.
3. always keep the ba-gua clean. If the glass or wood is damaged, it is best to change it with a new one. This is to enhance it's force and effectivity. Consult an expert on the date of replacement.

38. SPECIAL   MIRROR

Some people hang or display a special mirror in their living room. This mirror is concave in shape with a reflection opposite of the real image. For example, if a person is standing, his projected image will be inverted.

One has to know the exact degree of the mirror's concavity. Never attempt to display a special mirror inside the house without doing the following:

1. consult a feng shui expert if it is favorable for you to use it.
2. determine a lucky date and time.
3. Be sure to hang the mirror tightly.
4. always maintain the cleanliness and clarity of the glass.

39. THE LUCKY EIGHT TREASURES ®

Possession of the "Lucky-8-Treasures®" will act as a talisman to the owner.

It will help the owner to have peace of mind and good health; escape from hazardous events; make wishes come true; bring progress to business and occupation; possess both the powers of wealth and prosperity.

It will also drive away evil, ease anxiety, promote wisdom, and bring harmony to families. It is good to have one displayed in your home, office and factory.

40. HOLY GOURD®

The Supreme **GOD** joined by the Goddess of Mercy, had created this precious octagon symbol to bring harmony to our family, to have a friend to assist us in time of trouble, to attract fortune for our home and office, and to protect us from evil, witchcraft, calamities, etc., so that our lives will be filled with joy and goodness.

It is best to carry this symbol with us while travelling or visiting places.

It can also be hanged on doors, windows, bed's headboards, or even in the office such as above desks, vaults, and inside the vehicle.

41. THE TAOIST FORTUNE WHEEL®

This precious symbol was created by **GOD** during the ancient time to attract fortune and protect us. It has the power to save us from calamities, vehicular accidents, and free us from witchcraft.

It was stated in the early scripture that to hang this precious symbol on the wall, door, post and even inside vehicle, will protect our home and lives, and help us to prosper, too.

The following are the meaning of God's inscriptions within the Symbol :

1. eliminate calamities caused by evil spirits.
2. avoid being robbed, and thereby protecting our properties as well as lives.
3. promote harmony within the family.
4. lessen harmful effects of disastrous fire, earthquake, etc.
5. cure diseases caused by all sorts of evils.
6. cure insomnia caused by suppressing the devil.
7. protect and prolong lives.
8. save us from vehicular accidents.
9. cleanse our internal illness and prevent us from being harmed by the evil effect of witchcraft.
10. promote prosperity, increase wealth, and develop good reputation.

Owning this "**Lucky-8-Treasures®**" which I acquire from Rev. Wong of Sheng Lian Temple, really brings me lucks, prosperity, happiness peace and harmony.

GRACE GOBING

42. EPILOGUE

In the final analysis, feng shui is something between a science and an art. It is not a sort of superstition or something that belongs to a different religion. Besides arranging living quarters with optimal comfort for mind and body, feng shui also includes astrological and other "psychic" aspects. It affords a remedy for a person's bad fate.

By aligning or positioning one's self in accordance to the laws of nature, in the spirit of harmony and balance, a person's bad fate can be diagnosed and treated by good feng shui.

In practice, feng shui influences our daily life. Historically, it has been in existence for a long, long time in ancient China. Due to the limited number of people who can qualify to teach the subject, only a few are able to engage in the study of feng shui. Besides, the subject requires a long period of time to personally observe and gain experience in the field, before one can be endowed with a sense to appreciate and acquire it's technics.

It is a well known fact, however, that China had contributed a lot to the world through Her inventions like the use of compass, paper, silk, textile making and rocket. Mankind has greatly benefited from these knowledge. With this thought in mind, the author earnestly hoped that feng shui, like the other Chinese inventions, can be introduced and shared to all people in this world. Let all learn the secrets of this ancient science and apply it to their daily life so as to enjoy a healthy, happy life, and eventually use this know-how to promote peace and prosperity among mankind.

LUCK FOR DONOR AND DONEE

Gift giving is an eloquent expression of tradition.. It is a part of our culture. Almost every happy occasions involve giving and receiving gifts. A gift can be anything material, expressions of thoughts, symbolic .or spiritual. The value of a gift and the joy felt upon receipt of one are immeasurable items. Usually, together with the material thing we give, are the happy thoughts and good tidings we hope for the recipient. However, wouldn't it be nicer if you were to give gifts that can bring good luck to both the receiver and yourself?

For Filipinos, it is customary to give statues of Sto. Nino, which is believed to bring good fortunes to both the donee and donor. The Chinese, too, have a set of interesting ethics about gift giving. Hereunder are some of these beliefs:
1. giving the "Lucky-8-Treasures®" to someone moving into a new place can bring good luck.
2. it is good luck to receive the "Lucky-8-Treasures®" as a gift when starting up a new business.
3. as a wedding gift, it is good omen to give a set of "Pat Shien" to the couple for success and happiness. A gift of Buddha with children on His lap, will bring joy of "little ones" to the couple.
4. to help in the fulfillment of marriage proposals, it is beneficial to give a set of "Shin-na" or the Chinese basket.
5. to wish for good health and longevity for the elders, it is most ideal to give or receive a set of "Pat Shien".*

These gift items are mostly symbolic and of religious value, for this reason, these items become special and unique ideas for donors.

* Pat Shien - the Eight Lucky Saints

TESTIMONY

Chinese geomancy or feng shui has worked for innumerable people for many centuries. Today, it is still widely practice in Taiwan, HongKong, Singapore, Japan and even in some Western countries such as England and the United States.

Since ancient time, people believe that feng shui holds the key to everything anyone could possibly want: good health, happy family, good marriage, successful career, wealth, prosperity, good luck, and peace of mind... in its full scope. It is believed to help improve human lives and bring harmony to man and his environment.

The general idea, the aim of feng shui is to change and harmonize the environment, to improve fortunes of human. It operates on many levels, such as, practical and superstitious, sacred and common, folklore and religion, emotional and physical, linking all matters and minds into one unified theory. Sometimes, assessment of feng shui can fall short of logical explanations so that this subject remains a mystery to many.

In most cases, people have to hire the services of feng shui experts to define the location where the best ch'i flows in a landscape or a house.
Although each feng shui expert has his own approach, an authentic master demands that he act as an astrologer, topographer, interior designer, philosopher, psychologist, telepathic medium, and father confessor all rolled into one. Rev. Vic WongSengTian is one of the foremost masters adopt to this complex act. He is a Taoist Minister aside from being an authority in the feng shui subject. He has given remedies to difficult situations. Rev. Vic verified his secret ritual practice as mystical method of manipulating and correcting feng shui problems, these cures follow a transcendental,

irrational and subconscious healing process known as the intuitive method, or that which is outside the realm of our experience or knowledge.

For the past fifteen years since 1975, I have known Rev. Vic. I have seen several cases of marriages saved, careers made, sterility corrected, health improved and business prospered. I have known him to be sincere and he zealously attends to work in every instance. He is meticulous and exacting. Although always busy, he manages to explain important details and he is able to adopt his solutions to modern living standards. This enables us to follow instructions without being tightened up with stiff and or strange rules. He has been of great help to me and others for all the advises he had unselfishly given.

atty. M&Aun

CHARTS AND ILLUSTRATIONS

PREDICTIONS

1988 May

* The death of Republic of China's (Taiwan) President
* The big flood of People's Republic of China

1989 As published in United News of January & April respectively

* The Coup d' etat against then Pres. Corazon Aquino
* Late Pres. Ferdinand Marcos death in foreign land

1990 As published in United News of January.

* A devastating earthquake that will affect many big building

1991 As announced in Channel 13 " Mulat Isip" on last week of 1990

* There will be a war in Middle East
* The Country will have extensive drought
* A Major volcano eruption

1992 As published in Chinese World Newspaper of Nov. 1991

* Mr. Joseph Estrada to win the second highest position of the country
* Its not yet time Miriam Santiago to win the presidency
* A diffcult win for new Pres. Eddie Ramos

1991 to 2000 World big affair

* Western Countries economic and political situation will be a big problem. Friendship will be on & off
* Earth's temperature will change, there will still be many natural calamities, earthquake, floods and the like
* A nuclear power plant will erupt and will have worldwide effect.

195

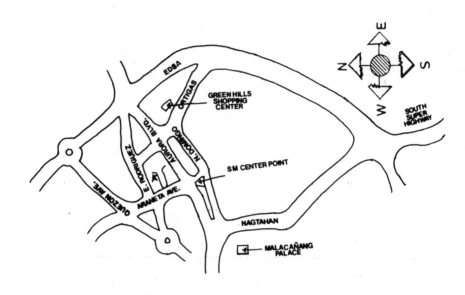

★SHENG LIAN SHIAN CHO TEMPLE

159 BAYANI STREET (BEHIND COCOBANK)
G. ARANETA AVE. (BET. E. RODRIGUEZ
& AURORA BLDG.)
QUEZON CITY, METRO MANILA, PHILIPPINES

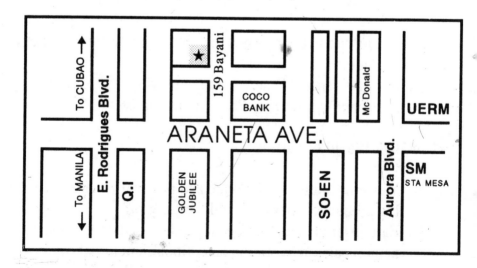

ACKNOWLEDGMENT

My deepest gratitude to the following persons:

Mary Sandra Uy

Hanabishi Phils. Inc. - Reg. Phil. Pat. Office

Arch. Jose Siao Ling

Mr. & Mrs. Jimmy Co

Mr. & Mrs. Robert Saez Co

Mrs. Susana Ang Co

Mr. & Mrs. Vicente Gomez

Dr. & Mr. Fidel Chua

Mrs. Socorro Ramos

Mr. & Mrs. Eddy Chua Villamor

Mr. & Mrs. Joseph Lim

Ms. Amy Aralar

Mr. & Mrs. Carlito Uy - Blackcatea ®

And other friends who gave their service and support willingly and wholeheartedly.

My gratitude also goes also to all the patrons and readers of the first publication of this book.

REFERENCES

I Ching   -   A Chinese Bible, devised by the Chinese sage, Fu Hsi, (B. C. 3322)

Tao Teh Ching   -   Laotze's book (B.C. 1122)

Huan Ti Teh Ching - An authoritive work, author unknown. The T'ang Dynasty (618 - 905 A. D.)

Teh Di Tai Chuan   -   Compiled by Kok Bok from China's most famous Feng Shui Masters. Ming Dynasty (1368-1644 A. D.)

Teh Di Sin Geng -   by the Ancestor of this book, wrote through his own experience with queries from all works of life

"Si Kho Chuan Su" - Encyclopedia

(above books are not copyrighted and are open for references.)

- During one of the speech of Grand Minister Vic Hua WongSeng Tian

- One of the activities of the Grand Minister's Sheng Lian Charity Clinic of which more than 200 of our brothers and sisters are of Bgy. Doña Imelda, Q.C. are the beneficiary.

\- The Holy Mass conducted by the Grand Minister for Heaven's intercession for peace and prosperity of the Country

FREE ADMISSION

***Exhibit and Explanation
are now on going about
Orthodox feng Shui Cure
and other fortune decoration
OPENS Monday to Sunday
from 8:00 am to 5:00 pm
at the Author Office***

201

Other items on exhibit:
- FENG SHUI PROSPERITY ITEM
- ANCIENT GOD TALISMAN
- AUSPICIOUS IMAGES

All items does not contradict with any religion, customs and traditions instead will counteract bad fate and maintain as well as enhance the current good fortune one presently enjoys.

Everyone's welcome
open Monday through Sunday
from 8:00 AM to 5:00 PM
or Call 711-27-14
Look for Rev. Vic and Naty

★SHENG LIAN SHIAN CHO TEMPLE

IF YOU ARE INTERESTED AND WISHES TO RECEIVE NEWSLETTERS ABOUT FENG SHUI, HOROSCOPE AND ASTROLOGY. SIMPLY SEND 12 UN-USED "ORDINARY MAIL" STAMPS TO:

ORIENTAL RESEARCH CENTER
159 BAYANI ST. G. ARANETA AVE.
QUEZON CITY, METRO MANILA, PHILS.

HOLY LOTUS®

The **Holy Lotus** was created by the supreme GOD joined by the Goddess of mercy, to bring harmony to our family, to have a friend to assist us in times of trouble, to attract fortune for our home and office, and to protect us from evil, witchcraft, calamities, etc. So that our lives will be filled with joys and goodness.

It can be hanged on *doors, windows, put on bed's box car* or in the *office* such as *above desk* and *vaults*, and it is also best to carries while *travelling* or *visiting places.*

Made of anodized plate that can be hanged or put inside our wallet.

Order Now!
Call 711-27-14
and look for Rev. Vic or Naty

159 BAYANI STREET (BEHIND COCOBANK)
G. ARANETA AVE. (BET. E. RODRIGUEZ
& AURORA BLDG.)
QUEZON CITY, METRO MANILA, PHILIPPINES

I am one of the lucky reader of your book and believe every bits and pieces of you book's contents.

- CECILE MOSTALES -
MAKATI, M.M.

I am happy to tell you that I read your very interesting book.

- **LYDIA N. LIM RAMIREZ MD** -
ZAMBOANGA CITY

I've read your book and I would like to congratulate you for your book is very well explained and the pictures are of big help to people like us where knowledge about FENG SHUI is limited.

- CRISTINA LU -
QUEZON CITY

I read you book and I found it very informative.

- **TERESITA DY** -
DAVAO CITY

I know that in one way or another, FENG SHUI will greatly influence our life.

- **OLIVE ANIS** -
MARINDUQUE

Congratulations po sa isang napaka-interesting at informative na libro.

- **SUSAN ABAYA** -
CABANATUAN CITY, N.E.

The book was explicitely explained with full pictorial details that helps reade specially one who has limited knowledge about FENG SHUI.

- **FERNANDO NGO (BUSINESSMAN)** -
BASA ST., ILOILO CITY

I feel very glad when I was able to successfully close an unexpected deal with Japanese. This happened on the day I brought home and displayed the LUCKY-8 TREASURES.

- **FRANCO CASTRO (ARCHITECT)** -
MEYCAUAYAN, BULACAN

NOTES

NOTES

NOTES

N O T E S